C000263640

DE[VON]
FOLK
TALES

DEVONSHIRE
FOLK
TALES

MICHAEL DACRE

The History Press

Wendy Dacre provided the main illustrations which were made as shadow puppet scenes on a screen and then digitally photographed.

First published 2010

The History Press
The Mill, Brimscombe Port
Stroud, Gloucestershire, GL5 2QG
www.thehistorypress.co.uk

Reprinted 2011, 2014, 2017

© Michael Dacre, 2011

The right of Michael Dacre to be identified as the Author
of this work has been asserted in accordance with the
Copyrights, Designs and Patents Act 1988.

British Library Cataloguing in Publication Data.
A catalogue record for this book is available from the British Library.

ISBN 978 0 7524 5505 1

Typesetting and origination by The History Press
Printed in Great Britain by TJ International Ltd, Padstow, Cornwall.

CONTENTS

INTRODUCTION

In 1988 I became a professional storyteller, having been inspired by The Company of Storytellers who were then touring Devon, performing and running workshops for Beaford Arts, our local north Devon arts centre. The company – Ben Haggarty, Sally Pomme Clayton and Hugh Lupton – were specifically telling stories for adults and I had never come across this before. I was spellbound, caught in a web of words, images and astonishing stories. Here was an art form whose existence I had never suspected but immediately wanted to practise. We signed up for all their courses and at the end of their tour we joined them in a public performance in the old cobbled inn yard of the George in Hatherleigh. After the show, over a pint or two on an outside bench, they asked us what we were doing and when we said we were unemployed at that time, they asked, 'Why don't you become storytellers?' So we said, 'All right then!', and we did. We got a brochure together and sent it to schools and began to get bookings. Two years later I was the storyteller-in-residence for the Beaford Centre.

Twenty-two years later, here I am with a book of Devonshire folk tales, the fruit of a rich and varied career in this large, diverse county; itself rich in the oral tradition, replete with legends, myths, fairytales and the popular fictions of a people close to the land. And what a stunning landscape it is! The stories reflect and are imbued with the wildness and danger of the moors, the ruggedness and treachery of the coasts and the remoteness and secrecy of much of the hilly, wooded and leafy lane-threaded countryside.

Devonshire Folk Tales is a new book of traditional Devon stories, some of them not previously published nor well known. One or two of the stories I have gleaned myself from ordinary people living here. A handful of them I have evolved over the years. Others are well known and have been anthologised in many previous collections but have here been given a new vitality, a fresh clothing of dynamic words.

All the stories are peculiarly Devonian, from the founding of Britain itself by Brute the Trojan at Totnes – he is supposed to have said, 'Here I stand and here I rest/And this place shall be called Totnes', and the stone he said it on can still be seen in Totnes High Street – to a Devon dialect version of 'The Three Sillies', printed in Ilfracombe in 1922. Additionally there are recent reports of haunted roads, of which Devon boasts a considerable number, told to me by personal friends and acquaintances, some of whom experienced the hauntings themselves.

Here then are tales of giants, devils, witches, ghosts, fairies (or pixies), spectral black dogs (of which Devon boasts whole packs), historical characters and a wide range of supernatural and natural phenomena, all exemplifying the vigorous and earthy nature of the Devon imagination down through the ages. It is a book of wonders to terrify and intrigue, and all the stories are set in an actual place you can visit, so it is also a tourist's guide to the folklore on the ground of this beautiful and fascinating county.

ONE

THE FOUNDING OF BRITAIN: BRUTE THE TROJAN AND GOGMAGOG

After the fall of Troy, when the Greeks took the city by means of the wooden horse devised by the wily Odysseus, some of the Trojans, led by Aeneas, fled the carnage, rapine and pillage and set sail into the Mediterranean, coming at length to the shores of Italy, where they founded a new city that would one day be Rome.

Aeneas's son Ascanius had a son called Sylvius, and when Sylvius's wife was about to give birth, Ascanius had his wizards surround the bed to predict the child's future and whether it would be a boy or a girl. The wizards duly intoned their tone-deaf incantations, drank their hallucinogenic potions, lit their noxious concoctions and examined their reeking entrails, thus by art-magic terrifying the young mother out of her wits. They pronounced that the child was a boy who would be the death of his mother and father, who would be outlawed, outcast and exiled and who would found a race and country whose power and fame would extend over the whole world.

Nor were the wizards out in their forecast. The mother died in giving birth to the boy, who was duly named Brute, and in his sixteenth year Brute killed his father in a hunting accident. The huntsmen drove the deer in front of them and Brute, taking aim, loosed a fateful arrow which whistled through the air and struck

Sylvius under the left pap. He died instantly. Brute's surviving relatives were uneasy at the proximity of a boy who had killed his parents, so the lad was exiled and made his way to Greece, where he freed the enslaved Trojans, numbering some 7,000, and in 320 ships this outlawed people, having no country to call their own, embarked on their greatest adventure, sailing into the Mediterranean and into the unknown.

On the misty morning of the third day, they came to the uninhabited island of Leogecia, which had been laid waste by pirates some years earlier. Brute sent a party of men to spy out the land and, after killing many deer in the forest, they chanced upon the ruins of a city, overgrown by trees and undergrowth. Among these eerie and abandoned buildings they discovered a ruined temple dedicated to Diana, goddess of the hunt. In the temple stood a marble statue of the goddess; intact, perfect, with bared breasts, raised bow and arrow, and features so lifelike that the men were afraid of her, for the eyes followed them around the clearing.

Returning to the ships with the venison, the hunters told Brute of the city and its temple, and that night he made his way alone to the place with all things needful for a sacrifice. He set up an altar before the statue, raised a goblet filled with wine mixed with the blood of a pure-white hind, drank from it and said, in thrilling, ringing tones:

> Great Goddess, Diana, forest queen, protecter of lost children,
> You who walk the maze of Heaven and the forest paths,
> Tell us what land, what safe home and haven we may inhabit,
> That we may build temples to you there, Great Goddess Diana.

Then he walked three times round the altar, poured out the wine and blood upon it, and lay down in front of it on the hide of the white hind who had kindly donated the blood. At midnight Brute slipped into the sweetest sleep he had known since killing his father and dreamed that he awoke, that the marble image of the goddess turned her luminous eyes upon him, that she stepped down from the plinth, the new moon in her hair, a sceptre in her hand, the morning star glittering at its point. Fixing him with her lovely green eyes, the goddess Diana spoke these words in a voice like a peal of silver bells:

> Brute, lost child, you sacrificed your father to me
> And you shall be exalted to the highest honour.
> You will sail from this sea, centre of the old world,
> Past the Pillars of Hercules into an unknown sea,
> Where you will find an island, the abode of giants,
> Sad remnant of a strong race but old now and past it.
> The Island of the Mighty will be your new home
> And you will found a race, the mightiest ever known.

When Brute awoke next morning, he hastened back to the ships and told his companions of his wonderful vision and with great joy they got underway, making full sail to the west in search of the island-home Diana had promised them.

They had many adventures, fighting off Moroccan corsairs and escaping from sirens, and in Gaul they found more refugees from Troy, led by a huge man called Corineus, 7ft high, strong and valiant, whose favourite hobby was giant-wrestling. They joined forces, sailing into the unknown sea, a fair wind behind them and on the third day they saw land. It was a place of mists and mellow fruitfulness, with a gentle coastline, richly forested, with red cliffs and sandy beaches. A soft rain was falling on their ships as they steered into the mouth of a river, tree-clad hills rising on either side as they rowed, slowly and wonderingly up this turning, twisting river, until they came to a broad, open place, the wooded hills lying back from it, a great dark moor in the distance. Here the river ran broad and shallow; ahead it narrowed, becoming unavigable so here it was that Brute decided to land.

He was the first to step ashore and, as he did so, his foot made an imprint in a large, granite rock lying on the bank and he said, 'Here I stand and here I rest and this place shall be called Totnes.' Actually he said it in Trojan or Crooked Greek but there, where the salt tide mingles with the brown waters of the moorland Dart, Totnes still stands firm and the stone that Brute stepped on lies halfway up the High Street, outside No 37. You can see the footprint and it's called the Brutus Stone, to prove the truth of what I say.

At that time the island was called Albion after the giant of the same name, son of the Celtic sea-god Manannan Mac Lir. He fathered a race of giants and they were the indigenous people when Brute arrived on these shores. But Brute wanted this land, for it was beautiful and bountiful and had been promised to him by the goddess Diana, so they drove all the giants up onto the high moors, where they sheltered in caves, and the Trojans took the land. But the giants were only biding their time. They gathered in a huge cave on Dartmoor, where they plotted their revenge, electing a leader for the first time, being natural anarchists – Gogmagog, who was 20ft tall. He could uproot an oak tree, strip off the branches like celery leaves and wield it like a hazel wand.

The Britons were celebrating the anniversary of their landing at a festival of thanksgiving to Diana at Totnes when the giants burst into the feasting hall and fell upon the surprised invaders, ripping off arms and legs, wrenching heads from bodies and gouging out hearts and entrails, Gogmagog laying about him with his enormous club. But the Britons soon rallied, fighting back fiercely, and the giants – huge, lumbering has-beens – could not dodge the British swords, spears and arrows. They fell in great bloody heaps until only Gogmagog was left alive and him they caught and bound, for Corineus had a mind to wrestle with him. For this they went to the place where Plymouth now stands, for there was much clearing up for the womenfolk to do at Totnes – burying the bodies, sluicing the blood from the hall, aromatherapy and new feng shui.

On what is now Plymouth Hoe Corineus, a giant of a man himself at 7ft high, faced Gogmagog, 20ft tall and ugly to boot, and soon they were hugging each other tight in the shackles of their embraces, making the very air quake with their heaving and gasping. Gogmagog broke three of Corineus's ribs – cric-crac! cric-crac! cric-crac!

Roused by pain and fury and suddenly imbued with divine strength from Diana, Corineus broke the giant's grip, heaved him up on his shoulders and ran to the edge of the cliff, where he hurled the monster onto the sharp rocks below, so that he was mangled to pieces and dyed all the waters of Plymouth Sound red with his blood. Thereafter that place was known as 'Lamgoemagot' or 'Gogmagog's Leap'.

The echo of this fight survives down the centuries to the present day. A Plymouth woman told Theo Brown, the late folklore recorder for the Devonshire Association, that the red earth of Devon was due to the county being formed from the body and blood of a giant, while in Tudor times, two giant figures were cut into the earth on the hillside of Plymouth Hoe. The Plymouth Corporation audit book for 1529 states, 'Cleansing of the Gogmagog 8*d*', and in 1566, 'New cutting the Gogmagog 20*d*'.

Alas, these figures, one of whom was surely Corineus, were destroyed when the Royal Citadel was built in the reign of Charles II; but during the excavation for the foundations the builders turned up a huge pair of jaws and teeth that could only have belonged to a giant.

Two giant effigies have stood in the Guildhall in London for centuries. The present figures replaced a pair destroyed in the Blitz of the Second World War, which in turn replaced a pair consumed by the Great Fire of London in 1666. They are now called Gog and Magog but Queen Elizabeth I would have known them as Gogmagog and Corineus.

After this great victory over the indigenous inhabitants the Britons colonised the country, calling it Britain after Brute, while Corineus ruled over Cornwall, naming it after himself. Later, Brute founded the city of New Troy on the banks of the Thames, which became known as the City of London. And so Brute, the slayer of his mother and father, outcast, exile and outlaw man, came home to the island of Britain and fulfilled the final prophecy of the soothsayers, founding the mighty race of the British people, and when he died, his three sons ruled the Island of the Mighty. Locrine ruled over Logria or Logres, which is present-day England, Camber held Cambria, which we call Wales, while Albanact ruled over Albany, which we call Scotland.

Thus according to that grand old fabricator, Geoffrey of Monmouth, in his *Histories of the Kings of Britain*, the founding of Britain herself took place in Devonshire, presided over by our tutelary goddess, Diana. You know it makes sense.

TWO

CHILDE'S TOMB AND THE LEGENDS OF ORDULF AND ELFRIDA

CHILDE'S TOMB

Childe's Tomb, a rough granite cross on a rough granite plinth, is not strictly speaking a tomb at all, though beneath it lies the remains of a barrow and a stone cist, or kistvaen, which have been empty for a long time. It stands at the edge of Fox Tor Mire, several miles south-west of Princetown and commands a desolate view over one of the widest and most treacherous bogs on Dartmoor, the one that Arthur Conan Doyle had in mind for Grimpen Mire in *The Hound of the Baskervilles*. Childe's Tomb is not a tomb but the memorial of one.

Risdon gives the story in his *Survey of Devon* of 1630. Childe was a Saxon lord in the time of King Edgar, Childe being his title, as in Byron's 'Child Harold' or the fairytale 'Child Roland to the Dark Tower Came', and he was 'a man of fair possessions', according to Risdon, owning much land in the Plymstock area. Childe of Plymstock was also a keen hunter who liked to hunt alone on the moor at all times of the year.

One day in the middle of winter, while tracking the deer out in the deepest wastes of the moor, he was overwhelmed by a blizzard that blew relentlessly for three days. At first he tried to battle his way through the blinding snow but with all landmarks gone, he went round and round in circles. Finally, when he and his horse were exhausted, he tried to wait out the storm; but the snow went on and on and on swirling around him, and Childe knew that death was at hand. In desperation, for he was a big man 'in the heat of his prime', as Risdon puts it, he killed his beloved horse, ripped open its belly with his hunting knife and crawled in amongst the entrails, seeking warmth and shelter from the deadly wind – but to no avail. The wind shrieked louder, the stinging snow drove faster, piercing the sodden carcase and Childe's life ebbed away. A week later, a pedlar crossing the moor caught sight of the horse's body and found Childe inside, curled up and frozen stiff. Nearby, scrawled on a stone in the horse's blood were the words, 'They fyrste that fyndes and brings mee to my grave / The priorie of Plimstoke they shall have'.

The pedlar brought the news to Tavistock, at which Abbot Sihtric and the monks of Tavistock Abbey were delighted, for it was well-known that Childe had ordained in his will that all his lands and riches should go to the church that buried him and this dying screed bequeathed Plymstock Priory as well. Unfortunately, the news of Childe's death sped almost as quickly to the monks of Plymstock and they were equally certain that Childe's lands and riches, especially the priory, should be in Plymstock hands.

But Tavistock was nearer and Tavistock got to the body first and started carting it laboriously back over the moor on a bier. The monks of Plymstock got wind of this and rode hell-for-leather round by road to the only bridge over the fast-flowing River Tavy, where they skulked most unmonklike in ambush, armed to the teeth. The monks of Tavistock heard of this too – the abbey spy network must have been almost supernatural – and they struggled several more miles upstream, where they erected a makeshift bridge, crossed over the swirling, snow-fed Tavy, and made it safely to the consecrated grounds of Tavistock Abbey. This bridge was thereafter called 'Guile Bridge'. The body of Childe the Hunter is indeed supposed to be buried at Tavistock Abbey, but how the monks of Tavistock got their hands on Plymstock Priory poses a problem, for there never was a priory at Plymstock.

ORDULF

Some scholars have identified Childe the Hunter with Ordulf, son of Ordgar, Earl of Devon. Father and son were buried in Tavistock Abbey, which they had helped to found. Ordulf's tomb became one of the famous sights of the abbey because it was so enormous, for Ordulf was a giant as well – 8ft tall. In 1125 William of Malmesbury gave an account of some of his feats:

> He was travelling to Exeter in company with King Edgar his kinsman. On dismounting from their horses at the city gate early in the morning, they found the door doubly barred and bolted against them. Thereupon Ordulf seized the bolts with both hands and with very little apparent effort broke them to pieces [though bolts are usually on the inside of a gate], tearing down part of the wall as

he did so. Then, warming to the work and gnashing his teeth, he loosened the gate with a kick and forced open the hinges on either side [though hinges are usually only on one side] with such violence as to shiver the door posts. The rest of the company applauded [no doubt uneasily] but the king pretended to make light of it, saying he must be possessed of the Devil's own strength.

In a wood near Horton in Dorset there was a monastery, now destroyed, which thanks to Ordulf's generosity ranked in those days as an abbey. To this place he used to resort in moments of leisure. There down a ravine abounding in game flowed a stream 10ft wide. Ordulf would bestride this stream and with a large knife would casually strike off the heads of the beasts that his retainers drove toward him.

'For all his size and strength,' writes William of Malmesbury, he died in the prime of life ('in the heat of his prime') leaving instructions that he was to be buried at Horton. But as he had directed certain legacies to be given to the church which housed his body, his wishes were frustrated by the violence of Abbot Sihtric, who carried off both giver and gifts to his own abbey at Tavistock. Later on Sihtric turned pirate, 'to the disgrace of his order and the discredit of the church', a vocation obviously more suited to his abilities.

ELFRIDA

Once upon a time the most beautiful woman in England was Elfrida, daughter of Ordgar, Earl of Devon and sister to Ordulf the Giant. She lived in Harewood Castle on the banks of the River Tamar, a few miles to the west of Tavistock, and the rumour of her beauty came to the court of King Edgar, who had recently been widowed and was looking for a wife and mother for his six-year-old son Edward.

King Edgar murmured to his most trusted courtier, 'Ethelwold, dear chap, ride down to Devon and bring me word of this Elfrida's beauty, whether she be fit for a queen'. Ethelwold took horses and rode down into the West Country until he reached the lovely fairytale castle of Harewood on its wooded elevation above the river. As he clattered into the courtyard, Elfrida herself came to greet him in the doorway. He was struck dumb by her beauty. With her long golden plaits, her eyes the colour of speedwell, young, clear-skinned, red-lipped and delicious, in her gown of pure-white silk trimmed with gold, she was the picture of a fairytale princess. Now young Ethelwold had brought his own heart with him down to Devon that day and he lost it there and then.

He forgot the weariness of his long ride down the A30, he forgot his friends' requests for clotted cream and cider, he forgot his loyalty to the king. He was head over heels in love and nothing else mattered. So Ethelwold wooed Elfrida for himself and because he was a handsome young courtier, impoverished but accomplished, he won her for his wife. But on his wedding night fear crept up behind him and tapped him on the shoulder. What could he tell the king? The king might not be best pleased with him for stealing his bride.

Then he had an idea. Making the excuse of important state business to his wife of a day, he rode back to the court and said to King Edgar, 'Your Majesty has been misinformed. Rumour has exaggerated the Lady Elfrida's beauty. She is fair but not so fair as to be worthy of a king'.

Edgar accepted his trusted courtier's word, while Ethelwold kept his marriage secret and spent as much time with his family as he could, keeping Elfrida in Harewood and Tavistock, where she was well away from the court. But rumour is a persistent hound, dogging the whispered tales to the king's ear – that Elfrida was even more beautiful than the tale-tellers said, that the king was deceived by his most trusted courtier, and that Ethelwold had seized the beauty for himself.

Edgar was determined to see for himself and ordered a hunting expedition to the Royal Forest of Dartmoor, commanding Ethelwold to prepare Harewood as his hunting lodge. Horrified,

Ethelwold rode hell-for-leather to Harewood, beseeching his wife to hide her beauty from the king or his life and their life together would be forfeit. But this was the first Elfrida had heard of Edgar's intentions toward her and she was furious. To be sought by a king, then tricked into marriage by a mere courtier! Why, the young scallywag wasn't even wealthy! She was the one with the money! But she concealed her true feelings beneath her cunning.

'Of course, my dear,' she soothed, 'we cannot allow the king to mar our great happiness together. I will find a way to disguise my beauty. Devon mud should do it'. Relieved, Ethelwold rode back to meet the king at Tavistock and brought him to Harewood.

But when they rode into the courtyard of Harewood Castle, there to greet King Edgar at the doorway was the loveliest young woman he had ever seen, with her long golden hair, her skin like cream, the bloom of the heather in her cheeks, clad in the costliest gown of light-blue silk to match her eyes. Edgar fell in love with her on the spot but disguised his true feelings under an aloof politeness and Ethelwold was much relieved, for it seemed that Edgar was untouched by Elfrida's beauty.

The next day, the Royal Hunt rode out onto the lonely wastes of Dartmoor and in the course of the day Ethelwold suffered a most unlucky accident; somehow he got in the way of a hunter's arrow and it was his lifeless body that was borne back to Harewood.

Loud was Elfrida's grief, but not too long. After the shortest decent period Edgar married her and she became Queen of England. So end all true fairytales. She bore Edgar a son, Ethelred, and she became stepmother to his other son, Edward; but as time went on she began to long for her own son Ethelred to be King of England.

Time passed, as it does, and this story now passes out of Devon into Dorset, but it will return.

Edgar died. Edward, his elder son, became King of England at the age of thirteen, even though some men said that Ethelred would make a better king, on account of Edward's outbursts of temper and violent behaviour; but Dunstan, the great archbishop and statesman, insisted on placing the elder son on the throne.

In AD 978, when King Edward was sixteen, he was hunting down in Dorset in the royal forest hard by the Purbeck Hills, when he got separated from his companions. Coming to the edge of the wood he saw, in the red glow of the sunset, a fairytale castle on a steep round hill. It was Corfe Castle, the royal residence of his stepmother, Queen Elfrida, in her widowhood. Now, although there was no love lost between these two, Edward was the king and trusted absolutely in his Divine Right, so as he was thirsty and hungry and the dark night falling fast, he turned his horse's steps toward the castle.

Queen Elfrida met him at the gate, for she had seen his approach. She was still a beautiful woman, richly dressed, her long, golden hair falling loosely down her silk-clad back, holding out a golden goblet of wine for her royal stepson to drink and surrounded by her servants in the darkening shadows of the gateway. Edward rode up to her as she greeted him with loving words, holding out to him the cup of wine. All at once her servants pressed close in upon him from all sides. One seized the horse's reins, one grasped and twisted his arm, while a third slid a long thin dagger between his ribs into his heart. The golden goblet clattered down onto the stones of the gateway, blood and wine soaked his hunting-dress – and Edward, uttering one anguished cry, spurred his horse away from that stepmotherly greeting, now slumping in the saddle, now falling.

Ethelred, watching wide-eyed and horrified from the darkness of the gateway, saw his kingly half-brother dragged on the ground by one foot in the stirrup into the woods. Elfrida's varlets ran after him, following the blood, shook the king's carcase free of the horse and chucked it into a nearby stream.

There it lay far into the night, during which time unknown hands raised it and bore it into the hut of an old blind woman who lived by the stream. In the night a great shaft of light shone down from Heaven, streaming through the gaps in the mouldering thatch and illuminating the royal corpse. The old woman awoke and saw the light for the first time in her life, hobbled across to the young king's body and looked upon his face, blessing God for a miracle and for a new saint.

People flocked from all around to see the miracle and the new, young, royal saint; so when Elfrida heard of this embarrassing development, she had the body removed and unceremoniously interred in Our Lady St Mary Church in Wareham, while her men burned the old woman's hut to the ground and doubtless got rid of the old woman as well. But the light still shone down upon the ashes and from them there bubbled a new spring, whose miraculous waters had the power to heal the sick and make the blind see.

So began the cult of St Edward Martyr, and a year later the powerful Earl Aelfhere of Mercia had the king's body translated in a solemn procession to Shaftesbury, where it was placed in a rich shrine in front of the high altar of the abbey church.

Elfrida fled to the seclusion of her old home at Harewood while her son, Ethelred, now wore the crown. But there were rumours and whisperings and malicious gossip all around her, while every day more and more stories of the miracles at the shrine of the new saint travelled down to Devon. Then three of her servants, whom she now shuddered to see, came to her insisting in no uncertain terms that she go to pray at the shrine of St Edward Martyr in Shaftesbury Abbey to allay the mounting suspicions of Edward's powerful supporters.

So she called for her swiftest, most beloved horse to be saddled and brought to her, but when it laid eyes on the queen it trembled violently and snorted and stamped and would not let her come near it. A second and a third horse were made ready but they too rolled their eyes and shivered and were as mad beasts at the sight of the pale and beautiful queen.

In the end Elfrida had to make the long, weary journey on foot, all the way from Harewood on the banks of the Tamar to Shaftesbury in Dorset, accompanied by a large retinue of her people to protect her from the populace, who spat and hurled abuse at the beautiful queen. Thirty years later Ethelred was forced to have his murdered half-brother officially declared a saint, for the cult of St Edward Martyr was a popular one. Ethelred also rebuilt Tavistock Abbey, which had been destroyed by the Danes, at his own expense as a penance for the regicide; but even so, Ethelred the Unready, or the ill-advised, wore a tainted crown to the end of his days, while his mother Queen Elfrida lived out her life as a recluse in Harewood Castle to the west of Tavistock, haunted day and night by guilt for her terrible crime and derided and hated by the English people. In fact, she lived unhappily ever after.

Three

Strange Waters: de Bathe Pool and the Wood Henge at Bow

The other day I went to de Bathe Pool again. It was a cold, rainy day, as it has been recently. I drove first to de Bathe Cross, then walked over two fields in the company of the land's owner to the pool. This is a curious hollow a little way up from the east bank of the River Taw, near the small mid-Devon town of North Tawton where we have lived for the last twenty-seven years. The hollow is roughly circular, about 100yds in diameter and 10ft deep, and when I went there it was dry despite the continuous rain we have enjoyed here lately.

But legend has it that the 'pool' fills up with water just before the death of a member of the royal family or great statesman, or a large-scale national disaster. It brimmed with water in the spring of 1914 and predicted in the same way the deaths of Nelson, Pitt, the Duke of Wellington, Queen Victoria, Prince Albert, the Duke of Clarence and Edward VII, according to a letter from Mrs Hole, the rector's wife, in the parish magazine of June 1910.

On 20 January 1936 the *Devon and Exeter Gazette* stated, 'Last week the Pool was reported filled and people regarded the omen as ominous [as indeed they would!]. The death of King George [V] on Monday night tended to strengthen the legend'. According to the same report, 'a crop of barley had been cut and stood in stooks. During the night the pool suddenly filled and next morning the sheaves were floating'. It must have been a bit of a shock for them!

In November 1951 de Bathe Pool started filling and it went on until February 1952, when King George VI died, upon which it abruptly emptied. This is according to a colleague of Theo Brown, the late folklore recorder for the Devonshire Association, who writes about the pool in her excellent book *Devon Ghosts*. I can add, on information given to me recently by a local informant, that 'Bathe Pool was out', as people round here say, prior to the death of Princess Margaret and that this is the only recurrence of the phenomenon since the death of George VI. It was quite dry for Princess Diana in 1997, and curiously did not shed a tear for the Queen Mother.

Thomas Westcote, the Stuart historian, wrote this about the pool in 1630:

> It was commonly observed that before the death of any great prince or any strange occurrence of great importance, in the driest time it would be so full, and continue to maintain a stream, until the matter happened that it prognosticated. And, as I have been informed it hath in these latter days been seen three times in the past thirty years.

So the legend of de Bathe Pool goes back a long time and may go back even earlier than the first Elizabeth; for in the thirteenth century the lords of the manor called themselves de Bathe, taking their name from the farm, as was common then for Norman usurpers trying to associate themselves with their stolen land. The name itself derives from the same root as Bath, the city, and Baden-Baden in Germany, signifying 'sacred spring or pool'.

Only a few yards from de Bathe Pool lie the remains of a Roman station called 'Nemetostatio' or 'the Station of the Nemet' and, following this clue into the mists of time, we find another reason for considering this area sacred or numinous, for the word 'Nemet' or 'Nymet' is Romano-British, Celtic in origin, meaning a

sacred place and it occurs all over this part of mid-Devon in numerous place-names – Nymet Tracey, Nicholls Nymet, Nymet Rowland, Broadnymett, King's Nympton, etc. It derives from the same root as 'nymph' and refers to a sacred spirit of place. In fact, in the Bow/North Tawton area there are two farms called East Nymph and West Nymph. A nymph, of course, can also be a fairy or elemental spirit residing in the very fabric of the landscape itself.

In 1980, during a severe drought, an aerial survey of Devon found the visible remains or post-holes of a large Wood Henge, 60 or 70m in diameter, in a field between de Bathe Cross and the village of Bow just three miles to the east, indicating that this area was deeply numinous or sacred to the Celtic tribes that lived here. Actually, the word 'Nymet' can also mean a 'Sacred Grove' and can only refer to the Wood Henge itself, of whose presence the Romans were obviously aware when they called their last station in the west 'Nemetostatio' or 'The Station of the Sacred Grove'.

A Roman road runs along the ridge above the Wood Henge and fades out in the vicinity of the station and de Bathe Pool. This was the furthest west the Romans got, apart from a small encampment or fort on East Hill above Okehampton. Were they prevented from going further or did they not care to? To the west and north lay only the 'vacua', the waste, a wilderness of deep, primeval forest. The area around the Wood Henge and de Bathe Pool was the last great clearing; so was de Bathe Pool even then a sacred and mysterious place, intimately connected with the destiny of Britain? Did it, perhaps, predict, by filling to the brim with water, the death of the first King Edward in AD 978? Did the pool even predict the death of Brute the Trojan in the same way? That could be why the Wood Henge was built here.

De Bathe Pool is certainly a curious spot – numinous, even a little eerie. Several of my personal acquaintances have had strange and frightening experiences on the roads approaching de Bathe Cross – sudden foul smells in the car they were driving, accompanied by acute feelings of terror.

I visited the pool once before, soon after we arrived in North Tawton, as soon as I heard about its uncanny reputation and I felt the strangeness of it. So did our Jack Russell, Tia. She shivered and whined and pulled away from me and ran all the way home. I found her waiting for me in the porch of our cottage.

The other day the pool was dry, despite the heavy rain we have had. I stood upon the rim, shivering in the unseasonable cold and wondered when de Bathe Pool would again be 'out'.

FOUR

LEGENDS OF SIR FRANCIS DRAKE — THE WIZARD

A GAME OF BOWLS

We all know the old chestnut about Sir Francis Drake playing bowls on Plymouth Hoe when the Spanish Armada was sighted sailing up the English Channel. There must have been great consternation, amounting almost to panic. The Armada had been feared for months. It was the most powerful fleet ever known, carrying the most powerful army ever assembled. As far as the ordinary English citizen knew, it was the end of the world, an invasion to rival the catastrophic one of the Normans 500 years before. Imagine how the people of Plymouth must have felt, looking out to sea and seeing that mass of towering sail sweeping over the horizon! They were probably running around like headless chickens, not knowing what on earth to do in the face of this apocalyptic threat.

But Drake, this stout little man with the red hair and pointed red beard in his ruff and doublet, his breeches, stockings and silver-buckled shoes, was perfectly calm.

'There's no rush', he said, as he picked up a bowling ball and prepared to roll it down the green. 'There's plenty of time to finish the game. The Spaniard can wait.'

FIRE-SHIPS

However, not many people know the reason for Drake's presence of mind. You see, he was a wizard, a highly advanced magician and he knew he could defeat the might of Spain anytime he wanted.

In fact, after this legendary game of bowls he went and quietly sat down on Devil's Point, which lies on the southerly tip of Stonehouse, opposite Mount Edgcumbe and just round the corner from Western King Point, a good vantage point from which to cover Plymouth Sound and thence the open sea. There he whittled away at an old chunk of wood with his old sailor's knife and every chip of wood that fell into the sound became a fire-ship that sailed out all ablaze into the Channel, where they played merry hell with the great Spanish fleet, warning the Spaniards in no uncertain terms who they were dealing with – the fiery *El Draco*, the English dragon who had already singed the King of Spain's beard at Cadiz.

WATER FROM DARTMOOR

But Drake was not just a master of fire; he could command all the elements. When he was Mayor of Plymouth, the laundresses of the city came to him one summer in great distress, for the area was suffering from a blistering drought, much as it does these days every summer in spite of the prodigious quantities of rain that fall, and these poor women could not do their work.

So Drake mounted his enormous black stallion with the fiery red eyes and rode up onto the southern slopes of Dartmoor, where he made the gigantic horse rear up and strike down with its iron hooves on the rock, which split open, releasing a cold, fresh, moorland spring. The spring became a stream that followed Sir Francis obediently as he rode back down to Plymouth, thus providing the city with its first freshwater supply. Actually, this story is based on fact, for when he was Mayor of Plymouth he did have a leat built from the moor to the city, which brought its first fresh water. It was called the Plymouth or Drake's Leat and ran from the River Meavy and its watershed for seventeen miles down into Plymouth, right to the sea's edge at Sutton Pool. Drake himself was the contractor and it was opened on 24 April 1591. There is even another legend that Drake rode ahead of the water on a fine white horse all the way to Plymouth; so we see in this the very line where fact finishes and fable begins.

DRAKE'S CANNONBALL

Drake the Wizard also had power over earth and air. After the death of his beloved wife Mary, he courted the wealthy and beautiful Elizabeth Sydenham, daughter of Sir George Sydenham of Combe Sydenham in Somerset. But Sir George would rather that the girl married Sir William Courtenay of Powderham Castle, a much more respectable match than the jumped-up pirate and upstart Drake, who was no better than a swashbuckling buccaneer, even if he was Vice-Admiral of the British Navy.

In spite of her father Elizabeth and Francis were betrothed, but then Drake had to go away for a while, sailing off in the *Pelican* to attack Spanish treasure ships on the Spanish Main. So before he went, he and Elizabeth exchanged solemn vows to be true to each other and Drake promised that if ever her father tried to force her into a marriage with Courtenay, he, Drake, would find a means to prevent it.

Off went Francis, for as yet he bore no title, and his expedition against the Spanish turned into his famous voyage round the world, the first ever undertaken, and three years later he was still at sea and everyone thought him lost – dead or taken – and all the time Sir George was constantly at Elizabeth to marry Sir William and no doubt Sir William was too. Eventually, convinced by the arguments that Drake was surely dead, she consented to the match.

The marriage was announced and the ceremony was due to take place at the Church of Stogumber in that lovely valley between the Brendon and Quantock hills. Just as the bridal party arrived at the church where Sir William was waiting at the gate, and just as Elizabeth got out of the carriage to go to meet her future husband, there was a fearful whistling sound from the sky and a red-hot cannonball fell through the air, hitting the ground right between the bride and groom. Elizabeth tore off her veil, cried, 'It's Drake's cannonball! He's alive!' and refused to go through with the ceremony.

A few days later Drake returned from his historic voyage and sailed the *Golden Hinde*, as his ship was now called, to London, where Queen Elizabeth knighted him on his own quarterdeck at Deptford and granted him a third of all the treasure he had appropriated from the Spanish, which made him a millionaire by today's standards. With his new-found wealth he bought Buckland Abbey from that other seafaring hero, Sir Richard Grenville, and married Elizabeth Sydenham. They had ten happy years together until Drake died of a fever off the coast of South America and was 'slung between the round-shot in Nombre Dios Bay (Cap'n, art thou sleeping there below?)'.

Then Elizabeth married Sir William Courtenay and had the best of both worlds. As for the cannonball, this was actually a meteorite and was kept at Combe Sydenham House in a place of honour in the Great Hall. There was a legend that, in times of great national peril, it would roll about making a noise like thunder, and that if it was ever taken away from the house, it would roll back to the porch by itself. Unfortunately for this last story, it has been in Taunton Museum since the 1950s. Strange that it should fall just where and when it did, though.

As for Sir George Sydenham, the countryfolk never forgave him for 'going against Drake', and decreed that he become a ghost, riding a galloping horse toward Monksilver, shouting wildly. He is dressed all in white and the horse is headless.

DRAKE AND THE DEVIL

Sir Francis was more than a match for the Devil himself. When he was converting Buckland Abbey into a fine country mansion the Devil, with a gang of lesser demons, carried away the building materials every night. One dark night, determined to put an end to this infernal nuisance, Drake climbed up into a nearby tree and kept watch. Presently the Devil and his demons appeared and started to carry away the stones. Drake crowed like a cockerel.

'Dawn's coming!' screeched one of the demons. Drake then lit his pipe.

'Aaaagh! It's the sun!' shrieked another little devil and they all scampered off, never to reappear.

THE WYVERN

Drake was now wealthy enough to have a coat of arms, so he incorporated the figure of a wyvern into it, to indicate his kinship with dragons; but this angered another Drake of the county, a real aristocrat whose own coat of arms sported a wyvern and who was furious that this upstart pirate should have one too. There was a great hullabaloo at court and finally Queen Elizabeth herself persuaded her darling Drake to drop the wyvern; but for ever afterward Drake hung the likeness of a wyvern upside down in his rigging as a calculated insult to his namesake.

THE CLEVER CABIN BOY

Drake was a jealous wizard. On his voyage round the world he had on board a cabin boy of 'uncommonly quick parts'. To put these abilities to the test, one day when they were sailing on the other side of the globe Sir Francis asked this lad what their exact antipode was at that moment. Without hesitation, the boy replied, 'Buckland Abbey, Sir'. Drake knew the boy was right. A few days later Drake put the same question to him. Again the lad came straight back with, 'London Bridge, Sir'. Amazed at the accuracy of the boy's knowledge, Drake exclaimed, 'What! Hast thou too a devil? If I let thee live, there will be one a greater man than I am in the world!' and so saying, he threw the boy overboard into the sea, where he drowned.

DRAKE'S DRUM

It is believed by Devonians that Sir Francis Drake, like King Arthur, will return at his country's greatest need and that each successive naval hero, such as Blake and Nelson, have been reincarnations of the great West Country seafarer.

It is also believed that Drake's drum, resting now in a glass case at Buckland Abbey, will play by itself when England is in danger.

FIVE

LEGENDS OF THE FITZ FAMILY

JOHN FITZ

Opposite the statue of Drake on the Plymouth road in Tavistock stands the gatehouse of Fitzford House, once a fine old Elizabethan mansion, and it was here that the Fitz family lived. John Fitz, a friend of Sir Francis Drake, was a London lawyer and a wealthy man with estates all over the south of England. He had married well too – to Mary Sydenham, undoubtedly related to Drake's wife. John Fitz did so well out of the law and marriage that he retired early to the family home and devoted his time to the study of astrology and other occult pursuits.

One day he was riding over Dartmoor in the wild region of the Blackabrook with his wife, Mary, when they lost their way. This was strange for they knew that part of the moor well. They must have been 'pixy led' or under a spell. They wandered around for hours, floundering through bogs and climbing hills until they and their horses were exhausted and the dark was beginning to come down on them. Then they came across a spring of fresh water bubbling up out of the ground and, being tired and parched with thirst, they dismounted and drank greedily from the spring, then let their horses drink. But as the cold,

clear, fresh moorland water revived their weary bodies, they looked around and their eyes were opened. They now knew exactly where they were and what direction they should take to get home. John Fitz vowed that he would honour the spring and make it prominent, so that other misled travellers would escape the pixies' spell.

Only a day or so later he had a small granite house erected over the spring and a granite wall placed around it. On the coping stone above the entrance he had carved his initials, 'JF', and the year when he and his wife had nearly died, '1568'. The well, the wall and the writing are all still there today, and you can go there and drink the miraculous water of the spring.

I did that once. I told this story to a magician friend of mine and he told me to drink the water by the tomb of John Fitz and his wife in Tavistock Church, under a William Morris stained-glass window. My friend Olli and I drove up to Princetown and had a drink in the Devil's Elbow. There was a thick mist lying over the moor. Then we drove to the stile leading to Fitz's Well and made our way over the moor, along the footpath and dropped down toward the Blackabrook in the mist until we reached the well. We filled two glass bottles with spring water, then drove down to Tavistock, parked and went into the church where we found that the Fitz's tomb was indeed under a William Morris stained-glass window. We laid our hands on the stone effigies of John Fitz and his wife Mary, looked at the stained-glass window and drank the water. Nothing happened. Except that when we went outside into the lovely spring sunshine, all the people looked bright and luminous, like angels, and we both felt intensely human and alive, excited by our adventure.

John Fitz was, as I have said, interested in astrology and when his son John was born in 1575, he drew his son's horoscope and, 'finding at that time a very unlucky position of the heavens, he desired the midwife, if possible, to hinder the birth but for one hour; which, not being to be done, he declared that the child would come to an unhappy end and undo the family'. (Prince)

SIR JOHN FITZ

John Fitz died in 1590 and Mary married Sir Christopher Harris of Radford, near Plymstock, while John Fitz the son, 'a very com-lie person', was brought up as a ward of court. He married Bridget, daughter of Sir William Courtenay (and Elizabeth Sydenham, perhaps?) and they had one child, Mary, in 1596, when her father was just twenty-one years old. John was now of age, free of all restraint and, for some reason, utterly free of any moral principle, pursuing a wild and reckless life at Fitzford.

One day in 1599 he was dining with his cronies at Fitzford and, having drunk a great deal of wine, boasted that all his land was freehold, when Nicholas Slanning reminded him that he held a parcel of land from him that he owed rent on. Fitz started up from his seat, told Slanning he lied and, drawing his dagger, would have stabbed the man had not mutual friends prevented him. Nicholas Slanning left and started home for Bickleigh but John Fitz and four of his servants rode after him, catching up with him as Slanning was leading his horse down a steep and rough descent. This must have been the wooded valley of the River Walkham, just a few miles south of Tavistock, and there all five men fell on Slanning with their swords. After a hot bout of swordplay, Fitz sheathed his sword and the matter might have been patched up but one of Fitz's men, a violent rogue called Cross, twitted his master, saying, 'What play is this? It is child's play. Come – fight!' Fitz drew his sword and attacked Slanning with renewed fury. Slanning fell back, his spurs caught in a root tangle and, as he staggered, Fitz's sword ran him through the body. Cross struck him from behind and Slanning fell to the ground and gave up the ghost. He was carried home and buried in Bickleigh Church.

John Fitz escaped to France, but later that year his wife and mother bought a pardon for him and he returned home, unrepentant, insolent and riotous. In 1603, at the coronation of James I, he was knighted simply because he was rich. Back at Fitzford he turned his wife and child Mary out of doors – they had to go and live with Sir William Courtenay – whereupon he entered into a life of total depravity, infecting the town of Tavistock 'with the beastly corruption of drunkenesse', he and his cronies, 'spending their time in riotous surfettinge and in all abominable drunkenness, plucking men by night out of their beddes, violently breaking windows… fighting in private brables amongst themselves… so as it seemed they lyved as, in time of old, the common outlaws of the land did'. According to Prince, the Devon chronicler, Fitz committed another murder about this time and he certainly all but killed one of the town constables.

But then, in the summer of 1603, he was summoned to London to answer a claim of compensation made by Nicholas Slanning's children for their father's murder and he set out on horseback, attended by one servant. His state of mind was alarming. A lifetime of debauchery had addled his brain and plunged him into a kind of schizophrenic paranoia. He saw enemies everywhere. He actually had enemies everywhere! The Slannings would hound him to his grave and the Courtenays wanted him dead. Each day of his journey to London found him more and more terrified.

He abandoned his servant at Kingston-on-Thames, convinced that he was working for his enemies, and rode on to Twickenham where at 2 a.m. he banged on the door of the Anchor, a small tavern kept by Daniel Alley, who put his head out of the window and said he had no room. Sir John insisted vehemently and went on banging, so Alley lit a candle and let Fitz in, even giving him his own bed and sending his wife to sleep with the children. There was no sleep for Daniel Alley or his family that night, as Sir John tossed and turned, crying out against the foes that pursued him and sought his blood.

Daniel arose at dawn to help a neighbour mow his meadow but his wife begged not to be left alone. The neighbour arrived and he and Alley went upstairs and spoke quietly about what was to be done. Fitz had finally fallen into a fitful doze but the voices awoke him and, fearing that his enemies were about to fall on him, he rushed out in his nightgown with drawn sword and ran Daniel Alley through the body, killing him. Then he wounded the wife but, in the growing light of dawn, he saw what he had done and stabbed himself twice. Other neighbours held him fast and took him to his bed. A surgeon bound his wounds but he tore away the bandages and bled to death. The only Fitz now left was his daughter Mary; but you have to wonder what Sir John Fitz's childhood was like, brought up by a father who was convinced by astrology that his own son would turn bad.

Six

Lady Howard

Lady Howard is said to run, in the shape of a black hound, from the gateway of her house at Fitzford to Okehampton Castle, there to pluck a single blade of grass from the castle mound and bear it in her mouth back to Tavistock, all between midnight and cockcrow and to perform this penance until every blade of grass is picked, when the world will end.

Another version has her travelling every night from Fitzford to Okehampton in a black coach driven by a headless coachman with a black hound running on ahead. The coach is made of bones and the skulls of her four husbands sit at each corner. If the coach stops at a door there will be a death in the house that night, and if My Lady stops to give anyone a lift, they've had it. There is a ballad, 'My Lady's Coach', almost certainly written by Sabine Baring-Gould. It bears all the Gothic colouring of a Romantic Victorian clergyman who also wrote novels:

> My ladye hath a sable coach,
> And horses two and four;
> My ladye hath a black bloodhound
> That runneth on before.
> My ladye's coach hath nodding plumes,

> The driver hath no head;
> My ladye is an ashen white,
> As one that long is dead.

This terrible penance, acted out for eternity after her death, implies that Lady Howard was a very wicked person during her life, who committed very wicked crimes. But, as we shall see, she was far more sinned against than sinning.

She started life as the only child of Sir John Fitz and, upon that person's dreadful death, was made a ward of court and sold to the highest bidder. In this case that was the Earl of Northumberland, who promptly married her off to his brother, Sir Allan Percy, when he was thirty-one and she was twelve. They never lived together, for Sir Percy caught a chill through lying on damp ground while hunting and died three years later in 1611.

Little Mary was now the wealthiest heiress in Devonshire and the Earl of Suffolk wanted her for his third son, Sir Thomas Howard. However, she ran away with Thomas Darcy, a young man of her own age, but this bridegroom died within a few months of their marriage. She was now married to Sir Charles Howard, fourth son of the Earl of Suffolk, and she bore him two daughters, but Sir Charles died in 1622 when she was twenty-six.

Mary Howard was now incredibly wealthy and an 'extraordinary beauty' at the court of Henrietta Maria, Charles I's wife. She was a friend of the Duke of Buckingham, who persuaded her to marry for the fourth and last time. This man, Sir Richard Grenville, was a protégé of the duke and a penniless but handsome soldier, and he was the worst husband she could have chosen. She must have had an inkling, for, before marrying him she tied up all her money, lands and estates in such a way that he could not touch them.

Sir Richard and Mary Grenville came to live at Fitzford where their first child, Richard, was born; but when Sir Richard learned, as he soon did, that he could not touch his wife's money or property, except what she was pleased to allow him, he was incensed and the marriage swiftly fell apart. As Clarendon says, 'By not being enough pleased with her fortune, he grew less pleased with his wife; who, being a woman of a haughty and imperious nature, and of a wit far superior to his own, quickly resented the disrespect she received from him, and in no degree studied to make herself easy to him'.

It was a real battle of the sexes between them. Sir Richard confined her to a corner of her own house, kept her from governing the establishment and installed his own aunt as housekeeper. His violence and language toward her was so bad, she had him brought before the magistrates, who ordered him to allow her 40s a week, whereupon he called her bad names before the justices.

He told his servants to burn horse hair, wool, feathers and parings of horse hooves and make the smoke go into her chamber through a hole made in the plastering. One night he broke down the door of her chamber and entered with drawn sword to take back the key of his closet, which she had taken away from him and refused to give back. He tore her petticoat and threw her to the floor, she being pregnant, and made her eye black and blue.

When it came to the divorce court, Sir Richard complained that she carried herself unseemly in words and deeds, that she sang unseemly songs to his face to provoke him, that she bade him go to such a woman and such a woman, that she called him a poor rogue and pretty fellow, and said he was not worth ten groats when she married him, that she would make him creep to her; that she swore the peace against him without cause and then asked him, 'Art not thou a pretty fellow to be bound to the good behaviour?' Then she said he was an ugly fellow and, when he was gone from home, she said, 'The Devil and sixpence goe with him and soe shall he lack neither money nor company!'; that she locked him into his closet and took away the key and it is true he endeavoured to take away the key from her, and hurt his thumb and rent her pocket.

Finally she fled from Fitzford and took refuge with the Earl of Suffolk and his family. Poor Sir Richard! He still could not get any money out of the estates or the tenants. Sir Richard then took the Earl of Suffolk to court but the judge found for the earl, whereupon Sir Richard abused the earl in such foul language that he was committed to the Fleet prison and ordered to pay £6,000 in reparation. This did not endear him any further to his wife, the unfortunate Mary, who, however, seems to have got the better of him at every step and given him every bit as good as she got. She was a powerful woman, proud, with a violent temper of her own and a tongue talented in insults – qualities she may have inherited from her father. Sir Richard languished in prison for some years, then escaped and fled to the Continent.

Then came the Civil War and all the positions were reversed. Sir Richard Grenville came home to fight for the king and was sent to Ireland in command of a troop of horse. When he returned he found that King Charles had no money to pay him, but that the Parliament in London had plenty; so he led his troop to London where he 'assumed the Puritan cant and nasal twang, recounted his great service, and protested his desire to quit the "Tents of Shem and cast in his lot with the righteous"' and desert the royal cause. Parliament was delighted. It welcomed this repentant sinner and convert with open arms and liberal hands, paying all his arrears and promoting him to a major-general of horse in the Parliamentary Army, with a regiment of 500 horse and the power to choose his own officers.

The regiment rode out of London with banners flying as far as Bagshot, where Sir Richard called a halt and gave the men a sermon on the sin of fighting against their anointed king, inviting them to come to Oxford and serve the royal cause. He was so eloquent that they all did; and at Oxford Sir Richard presented his sword and a well-equipped troop to a delighted King Charles. Parliament was furious. A price was put on Grenville's head, he was hanged in effigy and a Proclamation declared him 'traytor, rogue, villain and skellum', and he became known as 'Skellum Grenville'.

Now in high favour with the king, Grenville asked for all his wife's estates in Devon and these were granted to him. Only a fortnight after riding out of London he took possession of Fitzford House and plundered the place, squeezing all the money he could out of the tenants as well. The Civil War now raged back and forth and Sir Richard Grenville was made 'The King's General in the West', but he abused this position with such tyranny and cruelty that charges were brought against him and he was imprisoned on St Michael's Mount. However, when the army of Parliament drew near, he was allowed to escape and fled to France.

Lady Howard, as she now called herself, came down to Fitzford to find her steward dead and the house wrecked. She set about repairing it, bringing books, plate and furniture down from London.

Sir Richard Grenville died at Ghent in 1659, accompanied by his daughter Elizabeth. Tradition has it that Mary Howard hated this daughter of hers as the offspring of the plague of her life, and the girl had to be taken away from her mother for fear she would be harmed. When, a few years later, Elizabeth Grenville went to Walreddon hoping to be reconciled with her mother, Lady Howard, upon seeing her, rushed from the room and up the stairs. Elizabeth followed, pleading to be heard and loved, clinging to her mother's dress on the landing as Lady Howard went into one of the upper rooms. Mary then swung the door upon Elizabeth with such violence that it broke her daughter's arm. Elizabeth then departed to the Continent with her father and never saw her mother again.

Lady Howard died in 1671, disinheriting her children in her will and the local people never forgave her this unnaturalness. She was a woman of strong character, iron will and imperious temper and it is possibly for this that the people of Devon have condemned her to such a harsh fate in the afterlife.

Mrs Bray mentions the black dog and bony coach traditions in 1828, Dr Jago, the vicar at Milton Abbot, told Baring-Gould that she rode in a coach of bones up West Street, Tavistock, toward the moor, while an old man of the town said he had seen her 'scores of times'. A lady of Tavistock informed Baring-Gould that one night, as she was passing Fitzford gatehouse and just as the church clock struck twelve, she saw the hound start off. There are also modern accounts of the spectral black dog being seen in the lane leading up past Okehampton Castle. I myself heard two men in an Okehampton pub discussing recent sightings of the black dog, much as they would have talked about the weather.

SEVEN

DEWER

THE DEWERSTONE

'Dewer' is the name of the Devil on Dartmoor. He leads the Wild Hunt over the moor, pursuing the souls of unbaptised babes and hunting down evil-doers. He commands a pack of dogs called the Whisht Hounds, huge black dogs with fiery red eyes, controlling them with a whip made from the blackened tongues of gossips stitched together. They emerge from Wistman's Wood in the middle of the moor, just north of Two Bridges on certain nights of the year – Midsummer, Midwinter, May Eve, All Hallows Eve, the old witch festivals – and roam the moor, going about their unhallowed business. They are also to be encountered in the vicinity of the Dewerstone, a great cliff of rock in the woods near Shaugh Prior, just where the Meavy flows into the Plym. Dewer was said to lure travellers from Shaugh Bridge up onto the Dewerstone and then push them over the edge. In *Notes & Queries* (1850) a contributor writes, 'During a deep snow, the traces of a naked human foot and of a cloven hoof were found ascending to the highest point'. This refers to the belief that the devil had one human foot and one cloven hoof. The writer goes on to say, 'The valley below is haunted by a headless black dog'.

Murray's *Handbook for Devon* of 1879 says, 'and on stormy nights the peasant has heard the "whish hounds" sweeping through the rocky valley with cry of dogs and "hoofs thick beating on the hollow hill". Their unearthly master has been sometimes visible – a tall, swart figure with a hunting-pole.'

'GOOD SPORT!'

A Moorland farmer was making his way home in the dark after a late night in the pub at Shaugh Prior, when he heard the dreadful baying of the Whisht Hounds fast approaching across the open moor. With nowhere to hide and made bold by drink, the man stood his ground as Dewer galloped up, the slavering hell-hounds leaping and snarling around the horse's hooves.

'What sport, Dewer?' cried the reckless farmer.

'Good sport!' replied the Devil. 'Here, have a share of the meat!' and he tossed the man a warm, flaccid bundle wrapped in dock leaves and, with a Satanic peal of laughter, thundered off into the night.

The farmer, mightily relieved to have got off so lightly from this hellish encounter, hurried home to his cottage where he lit the lamp and roused his wife from sleep. Excitedly he told her of his meeting with the Wild Hunt and of Dewer's gift of meat – a large hare, maybe – as he undid the bundle. And there on the table, the dock leaves torn aside, lay the bloody, mangled body of their baby son.

BRANSCOMBE'S LOAF AND CHEESE

Further north, overlooking Sourton on Corn Ridge, stand two huge granite rocks known as Branscombe's Loaf and Cheese, while below them, to the east, in the steep ravine forged by the West Okement River, lie the Slipper Stones.

One day in the thirteenth century Bishop Branscombe of Exeter and his chaplain were travelling over Dartmoor to Sourton when a mist came down and they lost their way. The bishop lost his episcopal slippers too. They laboured along Amicombe Hill until they came to Corn Ridge. By this time they were starving and the bishop said to the chaplain, 'Our Master in the wilderness was offered bread made of stones. If the same were offered to me, I doubt I should have the fortitude to refuse'.

'O for some bread!' agreed the chaplain with a sigh, 'and a chunk of cheese'.

'Bread and cheese I could not possibly hold out against', said the bishop.

He had scarcely finished speaking when a moor-man came climbing up towards them out of the mist with a pack on his back.

'What have you in your pack, fellow?' asked the chaplain. 'Any food?'

'I have,' replied the man, 'but 'tis nort but bread and cheese.'

'Ah! Let us have some', said the bishop. 'We'll pay you well.'

'I want not your money,' said the moor-man, 'but you can have all of it if you get down from your pony's back, doff your cap to me and call me "Master"'.

The bishop was about to do so when the chaplain saw that the moor-man had one cloven hoof, like a goat.

'Save yourself, my lord!' he cried. ''Tis Dewer himself who tempts you!'

The bishop made the sign of the cross, the moor-man vanished and there on the ground lay the bread and cheese, turned to stone, and there they remain to this day to prove the truth of what I say.

SQUIRE CABELL

On the other side of the moor, near the town of Buckfastleigh, lived the evil Squire Richard Cabell, who was himself a great huntsman. He hunted the local maidens and when he caught one, he kept her locked up in his manor at Hawson Court, well away from his wife who lived across the valley in Brooke Manor, part of which he rebuilt in 1656, for this date is carved over the door. He was said to have sold his soul to Dewer and when he died in 1677, the Wild Hunt chased him over the moor. One of the great, black Whisht Hounds tore out his throat while Dewer sat on his headless black stallion and laughed. When Cabell was buried, the Whisht Hounds bayed around his tomb. That tomb can still be seen outside the porch of Buckfastleigh Church. It is a large altar-tomb, like a small house with a steep roof, a huge iron grille on the side facing the church and a small oak door on the other side with a large keyhole. Cabell was buried extra deep, with a large stone slab over him to keep him from walking. Even in the 1990s children from the town would go up to Cabell's tomb, walk round it thirteen times and dare each other to put their little fingers into the keyhole of the small oak door, where Cabell would gnaw their finger to the bone. Mind you, I suppose they'd be left with an excellent skeleton key. The children call it 'the vampire's tomb'. It was the legend of Squire Cabell and the Whisht Hounds that inspired Conan Doyle to write *The Hound of the Baskervilles*.

THE WHISHT HOUNDS

If you should meet Dewer and his Whisht Hounds out on the moor at night, you must lie flat on your face with arms and legs crossed and repeat the Lord's Prayer until they've gone. You must not look up, for if you see them you will die within the year. Ordinary dogs who hear the Whisht Hounds baying will die soon after; and in the 1890s they were heard at Okehampton, in the stables of the big manor house to the north of the town. Late one night the stable lads heard a ghostly baying of hounds up on Meldon Hill and, although all the horses had been settled for the night, they got very agitated, sweated buckets, almost broke out of their stalls and had to be rubbed down again and calmed.

BRENTOR CHURCH

Brentor Church, lying between Lydford and Tavistock on the western side of Dartmoor, stands on a volcanic outcrop of rock, like a miniature Glastonbury, and can be seen for miles around. In fact, it was said to have been built by a wealthy merchant who was sailing back to Devon and got caught in a violent storm. He saw the conical volcanic rock and knew then his direction home, thus being narrowly saved from shipwreck. He had the church built on the rock to give thanks for his deliverance. But Dewer, who did not like all these churches being built all over the place, interfered in the building. Originally it was intended to build the church at the bottom of the hill, but Dewer carried the stones up to the top every night. Eventually the builders thought, 'All right, if that's where he wants them, that's where they'll be'. And they started building the church on the top. Dewer then started carrying the stones down to the bottom; so the people called on St Michael to help them. Next night the archangel hid behind Cox Tor and when Dewer began to interfere with the stones again he threw a huge rock at him, hitting him right between the horns. Dewer made himself scarce and never came back. The church is dedicated to St Michael de Rupe, or St Michael of the Rock.

DEWER AS 'DIEUS'

The Dewerstone, however, leads us to Dewer's true identity. In Saxon times the rock was known as Tiues Stan or the Stone of Tiue, the northern god who gave his name to Tuesday. Tiue is a form of Tyr, the Norse god who put his hand in the mouth of the Fenriswolf and so lost it. Tyr is a later form of Tiwaz, a Germanic sky-god and a predecessor of Odin. The name Tiwaz is also related to Zeus and to Jupiter, who was originally Dyaus Pitar. All three derive from 'dieus', the Indo Germanic word for 'god'. Dewer is therefore a descendant of Tiwaz, Tyr and Tiue, and his name derives equally from 'dieus'. He is a Saxon sky-god related to Odin and later demoted by the Christians to the Devil and the leader of the Wild Hunt.

EIGHT

TALES OF BERRY POMEROY

The castle at Berry Pomeroy is approached down a long, winding drive through trees and is quite isolated. It is a gaunt, forbidding ruin and enjoys the reputation of being one of the most haunted buildings in England. My wife Wendy and I have told stories and sung songs there many times for English Heritage; so we have our own experiences to add; but we had better start with the main legends – the Lady in White and the Lady in Blue.

THE LADY IN WHITE

The Lady in White haunts the battlements of Lady Margaret's Tower – Lady Margaret was supposed to have been imprisoned in that tower by her sister Eleanor during the reign of King John, on account of an insane jealousy over one man. The poor girl was kept in the dungeon of the tower for nineteen years until she died of starvation. Theo Brown says that she must have had a remarkable constitution to have survived that long. She appears dressed all in white on the rampart walk near the tower and on the tower itself.

In 1913, at a meeting of the International Club for Psychical Research, it was related that a Mr King, an officer in the Army visiting his sister in Torquay, went to see Berry Pomeroy while on leave. He saw a beautiful young girl beckoning to him from the top of a high, ivy-clad wall. Thinking she was in difficulty, he climbed the wall to rescue her; but the masonry under his feet gave way and he nearly plunged to his death. He managed to cling to a narrow ledge, shouted, was seen and finally rescued. He was told that the damsel in distress was the phantom of a long-dead Pomeroy girl whose hobby was luring men to their destruction. As her appearance usually means death to the beholder, there is unfortunately a dearth of witnesses to her manifestations.

THE LADY IN BLUE

The Lady in Blue is deadlier. Dr Walter Farquhar came from Torquay to Berry Pomeroy because the steward's wife was ill. The castle was already a ruin but two or three rooms in the Tudor section were still in use. The doctor remained in an outer apartment while the steward went into the bedroom to see if his wife was ready for the doctor's visit. This outer room was large and ill-proportioned, with richly carved oak panelling aged black as ebony. The light was filtered through the chequered panes of a stained-glass window depicting the arms of Berry Pomeroy. In a corner to the right of a wide fireplace, a flight of dark oak stairs led to an upper chamber.

The door opened and a richly dressed lady in a blue velvet dress came in. Dr Farquhar arose and stepped forward, assuming she was visiting the sick woman, but the lady seemed unaware of him. She hurried across the room, wringing her hands in great distress, paused at the foot of the stairs and then hurried up. In that pause, the light from the stained-glass window fell on her face – a young and beautiful one – but, in the doctor's words, 'if ever human face exhibited agony and remorse, if ever eye, that index of the soul, portrayed anguish uncheered by hope and suffering without interval, if ever features betrayed that, within the wearer's bosom, there dwelt a hell, then those features and that being were present to me'.

As the lady disappeared up the stairs, the doctor was called into the adjoining bedroom to see the steward's wife, who was so ill she commanded all his attention. The next day, however, he found her much better and on the mend, and he asked the steward about the beautiful young lady in blue he had seen the previous day. The steward immediately became upset and kept exclaiming, 'Oh, my poor wife!' and told the doctor he was sure now that his wife would die.

Apparently, according to the steward, the young lady seen by Dr Farquhar was the daughter of a former Baron of Berry Pomeroy, who had fathered a child by his own daughter, who had then strangled the babe in the upper chamber and taken her own life. The apparition only appeared when someone living in the castle was about to die. The last time was when his infant son drowned in a nearby millpond. Even though the doctor thought his patient much better, she died the next day.

CASTLE MILL

The following tale was related by Miss E. Beveridge, who lived at Combe Fishacre. A South African friend was staying with her once and, taking her visitor out for a drive in her car one sunny afternoon in May, she turned down the lane to Castle Mill which lies in the Gatcombe Brook valley below the ruins of Berry Pomeroy. Half a mile down the lane they entered a strange, silent atmosphere in which even the Morris Minor's engine could barely be heard. In the field beside the track fowls they had never seen before, scraggy and long-legged, rootled in the mud by rough shelters of turves and branches. Turning a corner, they drove into a farmyard but the sheds were ramshackle, while the mill house was small, low and shabby, with tiny windows and ragged thatch. On a low wall near the mill stream sat a little girl of eleven or twelve. She was dirty, unkempt and swarthy, with coarse black hair. She wore nothing but a filthy sack with holes for her arms and legs and she crouched on the wall, her chin in her hands, glaring malevolently at the two women in the car with an uncanny, murderous hostility.

Hilda, Miss Beveridge's friend, said, 'I don't like this! Let's get out of it as quick as we can!' With a feeling almost of panic, Miss Beveridge turned the car round in the narrow farmyard and drove back up the lane as fast as she dared. As they made their way homeward they wondered just who were the ghosts – the evil little girl or they themselves, thrown back in time. Did the girl describe the strange vehicle that had appeared in the farmyard to her friends or family? Would she have been believed?

JOHN NOKES'S DREAM

In the *Transactions of the Devonshire Association* of 1879, there is an interesting story. John Nokes of Totnes dreamed of wandering around the castle ruins until he came to the fireplace in the remains of the Tudor section, where he looked up the chimney and saw an irregular bulge in the masonry. Chipping away the mortar, he found a secret hiding place, in which rested an iron pot filled with gold. He told his wife, who laughed at him and said it was only a dream; but he had the same dream the next night and again on the third. That time he woke up and, although it was after midnight, John Nokes dressed and set out for Berry Pomeroy in pouring rain and a howling gale.

On Totnes Bridge he met the local doctor, out on a late-night call on his horse. The doctor asked John why he was out so late on such a terrible night and John Nokes told him. The doctor laughed at him, saying dreams were irrational, not true things – mere wishful thinking. The doctor said he should go home before he caught his death, and that he could go and look in the morning when it was light and fine weather, if he still had a mind to. John Nokes took the good doctor's advice, not wanting to go against the fine gentleman, and went home to bed.

The next day, a fine and sunny day, John Nokes went to the castle at Berry Pomeroy and found the chimney and the hiding-place, but there was no pot of gold inside. Hitherto the good doctor was a bit short of money, but from that time on he behaved like a wealthy man…

DOGS AND CAMERAS

There are numerous accounts of weird experiences in and around the castle at Berry Pomeroy. Dogs and cameras do not like the place. Dogs often howl or go mad with fear, while cameras refuse to work and jam or spoil the film. Many films, when developed, come out completely blank; others show figures that were not there at the time the film was shot. My father-in-law had a photograph that he took of a ruined wall at the castle. When it came out the wall was not ruined but as it had been in Tudor times, and at one of the windows there was the clear figure of a man wearing a hood.

When we were telling stories at the castle for English Heritage, an American woman came up to me and complained that her camera would not work – the button could not be pressed down. I took her outside the castle and took a picture of her. The button went down easily. We went back inside the castle and the button refused to budge. She was incredulous so we repeated the experiment, with the same result. She was amazed – and actually quite delighted.

'ANYONE SEEN A GHOST?'

One day at Berry Pomeroy we arrived a little late, to find a group of some thirty people already waiting for a story. Just to fill time, I asked them if anyone had seen a ghost. One young woman timidly raised her hand and said, 'I think I have'. She then went on to say that she was just passing one of the window embrasures in the Tudor section when she saw in a flash, out of the corner of her eye but very clearly, a woman standing just inside. She was in Tudor dress, in a long, blue velvet gown with a gold bodice and she looked extremely distressed. I told the young woman that she had indeed seen the Lady in Blue. Later one of the custodians asked us if we wanted to park our camper van inside the castle that night, as the previous year we had had some trouble with amateur ghost-hunters. But I said, 'No way! The Lady in Blue has been seen today and she invariably presages a death of someone living in the castle. We'll be safer in the car-park'. The custodian laughed and said, 'I'll have to pass that one round English Heritage – Michael Dacre is believing his own stories!'

NINE

JAN BODACOTT'S STORY

Back along a while ago, the best storyteller on Dartmoor was Jan Bodacott. He made his stories so real, he'd have you believing in anything. For instance, when he went 'Baaa', and let his face go all woolly and vacant, why, you could actually see the flock of sheep being driven down the high-banked lane there under the trees and clattering over the little stone bridge; and when he told his chilling tale of the evil spirit that haunted the mill at Brimscombe Port, no one would go near the place, except for a bunch of publishers and they were never seen nor heard of again. But it was only in the long winter evenings, up at the Devil's Elbow in Princetown, that Jan had the time to tell his tales – for the rest of the year he was hard at work on his farm with his cattle, his sheep and his chickens.

One day Jan Bodacott noticed that his flock of chickens was getting smaller and he reckoned it was his neighbour, old Bob Harris, who was stealing them because once, when he'd gone over to borrow Bob's mower, he'd spotted a golden-brown chicken feather in the nettles there by the barn and he knew that all Bob's hens were scrawny little white efforts. But how was he to tackle Bob without making an enemy of him? Moorland farmers are always in need of their neighbour's help. Then Jan had an idea.

He waited until Bob Harris came over one day to borrow his rotovator and then he said, 'Yer, Bob, 'ave 'ee seen my big black dog yet?'

'Dog?' said Bob. 'You abm't got a dog.'

'I 'ave now', said Jan. 'I got him from the dog pound down Plymouth way, on account of someone's been stealing my chickens. I lets 'en roam round the yard at night, see. He's a gurt big dog, fierce and black, like the Whisht Hounds Old Dewer's s'posed to 'ave. Yer, look! Talk of the Devil! There he is, going along the ridge there, behind the barn!'

Bob looked and saw nothing – at first.

'Gor, you must be able to see him!' cried Jan, summoning up all his powers as a storyteller. 'There he is, look! Big as a wolf, black as the inside of Dewer's arse, with his gurt red eyes and his gurt red tongue hanging out and lolloping along, like!'

'Oh ah,' said Bob, 'I can see him now, sure enough! Yeah! Big, black, red eyes, red tongue, lollopin' along, like. Hoo-ooh! I'll keep clear of him all right!'

Jan Bodacott was amazed at himself. Why, he was such a good storyteller he'd just made old Bob Harris see a dog that didn't exist; and in the days and weeks that followed, the story proved a success. No more chickens disappeared. The problem was solved; but another problem was just hatching out.

One day Bob Harris leaned over Jan Bodacott's gate and said, 'Yer, Jan, I saw your big black dog today, runnin' up the road to Princetown. Lollopin' along, like, with his gurt red tongue hanging out. Proper fierce he looked! I was glad I was in the van!'

Now on the one hand, Jan Bodacott was pleased as Punch that Bob Harris believed so completely in the big black dog that he could even see it when Jan wasn't there; but on the other hand, he was angry and a bit disturbed that the big black dog was running up the road to Princetown when he should have been on the farm guarding the chickens.

And in the days and weeks that followed, it wasn't just Bob Harris who saw Jan Bodacott's big black dog. May Saunders from the Post Office had to jump back inside when it lolloped past, like, and snarled at her. Bert Wonacott met it in the copse up past the prison and climbed up a tree to get out of its way, it looked so fierce, while young Sharon Day saw it lolloping along, like, through the churchyard at dusk and she nearly fainted, for it turned and grinned at her and she thought 'twas the wolf that had eaten Little Red Riding Hood. The whole of Princetown was being terrorised by the beast. As May Saunders said, ''Twas worse than that there *American Werewolf in Plymouth*, or wherever 'twas!'

So Jan Bodacott decided to get rid of his big black dog. But he needed an audience – storytellers can't do it on their own – so he asked Bob Harris to come over and help him. He got Bob to hold open the back door of his old, red, ex-Post Office Morris Minor van, while he gave a low whistle toward the hen-house, 'Whoo-hoo-hoo'.

'Why don' 'ee chain the bugger up?' asked Bob.

'Dudn' do no gud', said Jan. 'He allus gets loose. He've got the power of Old Dewer hisself. I can't control him. Ah! Yer he comes, slinkin' round the hen-house.'

And Jan Bodacott made a great pretence of fastening an imaginary chain round the neck of an imaginary dog and tugging it across to the van, with many a 'There, there – he's a grand chap', and 'Just going for a little ride, Osama', until he got the dog up in the back of the van. Then he shut the door and said, 'Now say goodbye to Bob, old fellow, for this is the last he'll be seeing of you. It's back to the dog pound for you, I'm afraid'.

'Woof! Woof!' Bob Harris heard it quite distinctly.

Jan Bodacott drove down to Plymouth and wasted a whole day there, looking at all the consumer rubbish in the shop windows and treating himself to an immorally priced cup of coffee in Starbucks, but he reckoned it was worth it to put an end to the big black dog business.

When he drove back, dusk was falling as he turned into the driveway of his farm; but there he saw old Bob Harris waiting by the gate into the farmyard and a feeling of foreboding sort of lolloped over him, like.

'What's up?' Jan asked as he got out of the car.

'It's your big black dog', said Bob Harris. 'He must have got loose from the dog pound. Beat you back by about twenty minutes. That's when I saw him runnin' past my place, lollopin' along, like, with his red tongue hanging out an' his red eyes glarin' through the gloom.'

Jan was furious. For a shred of Golden Virginia he'd've punched old Bob Harris in the mouth.

'Bob Harris, you're a liar!' he shouted. 'I left thick big black dog behind a big steel fence. He couldn't have got loose!'

'Oh, a liar, am I?' yelled Bob Harris, going red with rage himself. 'We'll soon see who the liar is, Jan Bodacott!' And he stomped off, back to his own farm.

And in the days and weeks that followed, the big black dog proved larger than life and twice as vicious. He'd really got it in for people now. He lolloped right into the Post Office and trapped May Saunders behind the grille for half an hour while he wolfed down all the chocolates on the sweet shelves; he was only driven out by a couple of extra-hard screws (or prison-officers).

Bert Wonacott was chased down from the copse above the prison and had to take refuge in the prison itself. 'Only safe place on Dartmoor!' he declared. Young Sharon Day had her My Little

Pony Punishment Block ripped to pieces in the recreation ground and she was never the same maid again. Not only that, but Jan Bodacott and Bob Harris were no longer friends, so Jan might just as well have accused Bob of stealing his chickens in the first place.

Jan stayed away from Princetown as much as he could now, but he still had to get his Golden Virginia once a week and one day he was just coming out of the Post Office when Bob Harris's old, red, ex-Post Office Morris Minor van screeched to a halt beside Jan's and Bob got out, shaking with fury, his left hand dripping blood onto the road.

'Your bleddy dog just bit me!' he barked. Jan went over and looked at the wound.

'Looks like an axe-cut to me', he said.

'Axe-cut?' yelled Bob Harris. 'Look! D'you think I don't know it when a bleddy big black dog jumps over my fence when I'm chopping wood and damn near bites my hand off?'

By this time a crowd had gathered and everyone got angry with Jan Bodacott and his big black dog. They said the both of them should be run out of the parish, banished from Dartmoor even. Jan was frightened.

'Look yer,' he said, 'this has gone beyond a joke. I ab'm got a big black dog. I never had a big black dog. I never wants a big black dog. Not ever! It was all just a story I made up.'

'Hah!' cried Bob Harris. 'A story he made up? That's a likely story, that is! Now he's telling stories, trying to get out of it! Sayin' he ain't got no big black dog! Why, I've seen it with me own eyes, loads of times, sort of lollopin' along, like, with its red tongue hangin' out. And just now it damn near bit my hand off!'

'I've seen it too!' cried May Saunders.

'So have I!' said Bert Wonacott.

'So've I!' said Sharon Day.

'Right!' said Jan. 'I've had enough! Everyone back to my farm. I needs witnesses.' So they all piled into Jan's and Bob's old, red, ex-Post Office Morris Minor vans and went to Jan's farm, where Jan gave Bob two of his plumpest pullets by way of compensation for the injury to his hand and said, 'Now wait yer, you lot'. He went into the house and came out with his shotgun. He gave a low whistle toward the hen-house, 'Whoo-hoo-hoo!' and then, as the tension mounted and they all stared expectantly, Jan summoned up all his powers as a storyteller and, pointing dramatically, ex-claimed, 'Ah! There he is, look! Slinkin' round the hen-house, sort of lollopin' along, like, real slow, with his red tongue hangin' out, his red eyes a-glarin' guiltily, tail twixt his legs – he knaws zum-mat's up – and a real hangdog look!'

And everyone there saw that big black dog just as plainly and as vividly as you now see it in your own mind's eye. Jan Bodacott lifted the gun to his shoulder, aimed it carefully – at nothing, let's be quite clear about that – and squeezed the trigger. Bang! May Saunders screamed, Bert Wonacott flinched and Sharon Day fainted away into a heap of manure.

There!' sobbed Jan, brushing away a tear in spite of himself. 'I've made an end of my big black dog. Are we all agreed on that?' And everyone agreed that the big black dog was dead; and when they'd all been driven back to Princetown, Bob Harris came back to Jan's farm and helped Jan bury it. And that really was the end of Jan Bodacott's big black dog. Or was it?

TEN

THE DEVIL AT WIDECOMBE

Widecombe is the best-known village on Dartmoor due to that absurd 'folk song', 'Widecombe Fair', almost certainly the work of the Revd Sabine Baring-Gould. On account of this song you want to avoid the place in the summertime, when hordes of sightseers of all nationalities descend on the village in cars and coaches, on motorbikes, bicycles and on foot, swarming over the tea-rooms, wishing wells, gift shops and plastic pixy ghettoes like horseflies on a cowpat and clogging the narrow lanes leading down to this 'honeypot', for Widecombe is not an easy place to get to, lying in a steep valley hemmed in on all sides by the wild uplands of the high moor. This valley is known as 'the valley of thunderstorms', for it attracts them as the village attracts grockles, and on Sunday 21 October 1638 the worst thunderstorm of recorded history swept down the valley and hit Widecombe Church, called the 'Cathedral of the Moor' on account of its fine, lofty tower topped by four large, pointed pinnacles.

The Revd George Lyde was taking the afternoon service when the storm struck, causing fearful damage and killing at least four people and injuring sixty-two. In the words of an eye-witness:

> There was terrible and fearful thunder, like the noise of many guns, accompanied by dreadful lightning, to the great amazement of the

people, the darkness still increasing, that they could not see each other. Then an extraordinary flame passed right through the church, filling it with the loathsome smell of brimstone and a great ball of fire fell through the roof.

It was terrifying, as if the Devil himself, or Dewer, as he is called on Dartmoor, had descended on the church. There are contemporary accounts of the disaster, including one by Richard Hill, the village schoolmaster, in wonderfully bad verse on four wooden boards hanging up in the church.

There were some pretty strange injuries and incidents. A large beam crashed down between the parson and the clerk, yet neither man was touched. The beam was all scorched and withered and alight with blue and green flames. The parson's wife was scorched black in the pew where she sat but her little child sitting beside her was unhurt. One woman, who tried to run out of the church, was so horribly burned that she died that night. A man was so badly scorched by the ball of fire that he died after fourteen days of the most intolerable agony, yet his clothes were barely touched. Another man had all the money in his purse melted into an unusable lump but the purse itself was undamaged. Yet another man had his head cloven, his skull split into three pieces and his brains thrown whole onto the floor – but the hair of his head stuck fast to the pillar behind him, where it remained a woeful sight for a long time afterward. A child was seen to walk up the aisle as the flame passed down and was not hurt at all.

At the height of this apocryphal storm, one of the pinnacles of the tower crashed down through the roof, injuring many people. In all this chaos and destruction, most of the congregation wanted to run outside but the Revd Lyde firmly restrained them, saying, 'Let us make an end of prayer. It were better that we died here than in another place'. He may have prevented a panic that could have killed even more people, or caused injuries that a swift evacuation would have avoided. Although Richard Hill the schoolmaster evidently considered the catastrophe an act of God, a far different legend rapidly accrued to this well-documented occurrence. This was the work of the Devil himself!

Twenty years earlier a wild young man of the parish called Jan Reynolds had made a pact with Dewer, for Jan was a ne'er-do-well, a scallywag who was always drinking and playing cards and consorting with loose women so, of course, he was always short of money. He sold his soul to Dewer for a never-failing purse and swore that the Evil One could claim his soul the moment he found him asleep in church. Jan reckoned that wouldn't happen, as he rarely went to church anyway, even though that was frowned on then – and in any case the pews were hard and there were always plenty of pretty girls to look at.

But on Sunday 21 October 1638 Jan was tired. He'd been in the pub the night before, drinking and whoring and playing cards as usual, and now his family, shocked at his wild behaviour, had forced him to attend the afternoon service. He hadn't got home until three o'clock that morning and by the time the parson was droning on with his sermon Jan was fast asleep, snoring gently, his pack of playing cards – the Devil's Pictures – half-hanging out of his waistcoat pocket.

A short time before, some local farmers were enjoying a lunch-time pint in the Tavistock Inn at Poundsgate. All at once they heard the sound of galloping hooves drumming up the road from Ashburton and a tall, dark stranger dressed all in black rode up on a huge, jet-black mare. He dismounted and strode into the inn, where he demanded ale in a deep, cultured voice. The men were in awe of him but when the landlady brought him the ale, he paid for it in gold, far more than the price of a pint, so the landlady was minded to be civil with him, even though when he smiled she caught a glimpse of very long, sharp teeth. He tipped back the tankard of ale, a quart measure, and downed it in one long draught – and everyone in that room heard the liquor sizzle and hiss as it ran down his throat, just as if it were being poured over red-hot iron. He handed the empty and rather warm mug back to the landlady with a cynical smile and asked her the way to Widecombe. She told him in a scared, faltering voice and he strode outside, mounted his horse and thundered off in that direction. Everyone in the Tavistock Inn was stunned, especially when the landlady turned to gather up the gold on the bar-top, only to grasp a pile of reddish-gold autumn leaves.

'That were Dewer hisself!' she gasped.

'Ah!' said old Bob Harris. 'I didn't think he comed from round yer – everyone d'know where Widecombe be to.'

Dewer, the Evil Rider, the Wild Huntsman, galloped onward, riding now on the wings of a gigantic thunderstorm as he soared down into the Widecombe valley and tethered his great black mare to one of the pinnacles of the church tower. Then he crashed down through the roof in a swirling ball of fire and regarded with triumph the still sleeping Jan Reynolds, the wicked cards still poking out of his pocket.

Crying, 'Wakey, wakey!', Dewer seized the wretch, dashed his brains out on the pillar behind him, slung the limp body over his back and flew up through the church again to his horse, who dislodged the pinnacle with a mighty kick as Dewer threw himself onto her back, sending it crashing down into the church as he rode off into the storm-wracked sky in a hail of fire and brimstone.

The last that was ever seen of wicked Jan Reynolds was when Dewer and his black mare were riding across the sky near the Warren House Inn to the north. The great storm accompanied them like hellish outriders and the drinkers came out to see what all the racket was, and they clearly saw the black horse and its black rider, and the body that Dewer bore. Even as they watched, horror-struck, the four aces from the pack in Jan's pocket fluttered to the ground, where they were at once transformed into 'newtakes', small stone enclosures, and they can be seen there to this day – they are known as the Ace Fields.

The belief that the Widecombe church disaster of 1638 was the work of the Devil is strong on Dartmoor, rooted in the very ground. When asked by his teacher where the Devil was to be found, a small boy of Postbridge, just down the road from the Warren House Inn, replied, 'If you please, ma'am, he lives to Widecombe'.

ELEVEN

CRANMERE BENJIE

Cranmere Pool is a peat bog lying some five miles south of Okehampton in a hollow of rough, marshy ground and is one of the
most godforsaken places on the face of the earth. A few yards
away the River Okement, which gives Okehampton its name,
starts its journey, and in the nineteenth century Cranmere Pool
was reserved as the dwelling place of unruly ghosts, 'a great penal
settlement for refractory spirits' as *Notes & Queries* of 1851 has it.
Its name derives from 'Crow's Mere', so perhaps it once had more
water in it than it does now.

One of the pool's most infamous ghosts was Cranmere Benjie,
or Bengie Geare, a real person by the name of Benjamin Gayer
who was five times Mayor of Okehampton in the seventeenth century and who died in 1701. There is a memorial plaque in Latin to
him in the vestry of the parish church, but his grave is not marked.
On a wall in St James' Street there were once carved, high up, the
letters 'BG' and the date 1696, but the wall has been knocked
down to make way for a betting shop and an off-license, a move of
which Benjamin Gayer would probably have approved.

For Benjamin Gayer was a wealthy merchant of the town and
owned a public house, but he got into financial difficulties and became desperate for money. It was possible that his merchant ships

were taken by corsairs or otherwise lost at sea, for Mr Gayer was in charge of a large fund of money set aside to ransom English sailors captured by Barbary pirates and it was thought that he now began to embezzle these funds for his own purposes, and that it was guilt for this crime that refused to let him rest when he was dead, while even more fanciful stories suggested that he robbed and killed the guests staying at his inn.

For whatever reason, Benjamin was singularly unquiet after his death. He haunted his inn and the whole of Okehampton so badly with his loud cries and lamentations that his fellow Ock-etonians went to the vicar and insisted that he 'lay' the ghost. The vicar must have known his job, for he harried the former mayor out to Cranmere Pool in the wastes of the northern morass and ordered him to bale out the pool with a sieve. But after many years of this wearisome and thankless business Benjie, as he was now called, waited until an unsuspecting sheep wandered too close, caught it, killed it, skinned it (with his teeth I should think), then lined the sieve with the sheepskin and baled out the pool so fast that Okehampton was flooded. Leaping down on the heels of the flood came Cranmere Benjie, who haunted the town worse than before, having been made wild and mad by his lonely and boring exile on the moor.

Several more learned parsons were brought in and they suc-ceeded in driving the ghost up to Cranmere Pool again, where they set him the time-honoured task of making bundles of sand, tied together with ropes of sand. Apparently he managed this as well, for he appeared in Okehampton yet again, weeping and wailing even louder and more annoyingly than ever.

This time the sleepless Ocketonians appealed to the archdea-con of the diocese and he dispatched no less than twenty-four clergymen to exorcise the evil spirit. They gathered together at his inn and uttered prayers in English, Latin, Greek and Hebrew, but Benjie defied them all until the twenty-fourth addressed him in Arabic. Benjie was so startled at hearing Arabic in Okehampton – and maybe his conscience was thereby pricked on account of the

sailors imprisoned by the Turks – that all the fight went out of him and he cried out, 'Now thou art come, I must be gone!'

The good clergymen then transformed him into a black colt, fitting him with an unused bit and bridle and commanding a simple servant boy, who was given Holy Communion, to ride the colt to Cranmere Pool, dismount, take off the bridle and walk quickly back to Okehampton without once looking behind him. All went well until the lad slipped the bridle off, then curiosity got the better of him and he glanced back to see the colt plunge into the bog in the shape of a ball of fire. But before it did, it kicked out one of its back hooves and knocked out one of the boy's eyes. So a sacrifice was made and Benjie was once more bound to the desolate pool, which is said to be haunted still by his spirit, either in the form of a black pony or a black dwarf.

A later tradition of Cranmere Benjie persisted in Okehampton until the turn of the nineteenth century. It was said that you could raise his turbulent spirit if you walked round a table three times widdershins (anti-clockwise), reciting each time the inspired incantation:

Benjie Geare! Benjie Geare!
If thou art near, do thou appear!

An old gentleman was persuaded to enact this trite little ritual one Christmas by his nephews and nieces as a party trick, but when he got halfway through the third recital such a terrific thunderstorm burst over the town that the old man nearly had a heart attack and could never be persuaded to practice necromancy again. But when you are next in Okehampton, why not give it a try?

Twelve

The Hairy Hands
of Postbridge

In March 1921 Dr Helby, the Dartmoor Prison doctor, was asked to go to Postbridge to attend an inquest on a man named French, who had been thrown from his horse and trap, and killed. Dr Helby took his motorcycle and sidecar, in which Mrs Helby and the two young daughters of the prison's deputy governor went along for the ride.

Near the gateway of Archerton Drive, on the hill going down into Postbridge, the motorcycle suddenly swerved off the road, pitching Dr Helby into the ditch where he broke his neck. Mrs Helby and the children were flung onto the verge, still in the sidecar, but not seriously hurt. People from Postbridge looked after them and brought them home.

On the same day a Dr Adkin of Exmouth, as a small boy, was holidaying with his parents at Cherrybrook Farm, two miles south-west of Archerton. They were driving along the B3212 towards Postbridge when they saw that an accident had taken place a short distance ahead. Dr Adkin's father, a doctor himself, stopped the car, told his family to stay in it and went to help. He found Dr Helby dead and Mrs Helby distraught, but she was able to say that as they approached the place, her husband had cried out something about 'hair' and 'hands', and that he was losing control of the machine.

Later that year, on 26 August, a dull and foggy Friday, a young Army officer staying at Penlee Farm in Postbridge offered to ride his motorcycle to Princetown on an errand for his hostess. He returned within the hour, white and shaken, to say that not far beyond the clapper bridge, on that selfsame stretch of the B3212 going uphill out of the village, he had felt his own hands gripped by two rough, hairy hands which made every effort to throw him off the machine. He tried to fight them but they were too strong and wrenched him off the road into the shallow ditch bordering Bellever Forest. Being an experienced rider, he managed to slow the motorcycle down so he only suffered shock and some minor scratches.

These two accounts were related to Theo Brown, the late folklore recorder for the Devonshire Association, by Mrs Battiscombe, the widow of Dr Helby's successor at Dartmoor Prison.

The stories, which were reported in the *Daily Mail* on 14 and 15 October 1921, caused a sensation at the time, along with an account given by the driver of a charabanc – an open-topped motor coach – which had mounted the bank and plunged into the ditch at exactly the same spot. Fortunately no one was badly hurt but the driver said, 'I felt hairy hands pull the wheel toward the Lakehead side', that is to say, toward Lakehead Hill, which is part of Bellever Forest on the left-hand side of the road. No one listened to him at the time. The camber of the road was blamed and council road men were soon there improving it, but it did not stop the accidents or explain the hairy hands or stop them from being seen.

Theo Brown, in her book *Devon Ghosts*, states that her mother actually saw one of the hairy hands while caravanning on the moor near Postbridge in 1924. The family had camped among the ruins of Powder Mills, an old gunpowder factory about a mile to the south-west of the haunted stretch of road.

It was a cold, moonlit night and everyone was asleep except Theo's mum, who was lying in a bunk at the side of the caravan facing a small window at the end, beneath which her husband lay fast asleep in his bunk. She had awoken suddenly to an intense sensation of fear, danger and the awareness of some terrible power that menaced them.

As she looked toward the little window at the end of the caravan, she saw something moving on it and made out the fingers
and palm of a large hand with a lot of black hair on the joints
and the back, clawing its way up to the top of the window, which
was partly open. She knew at once that it was no ordinary human hand and that it wanted to harm her sleeping husband, and
indeed all of them. She also knew that it could not be hurt by any
ordinary human agency, such as a blow or a shot. She made the
sign of the cross and prayed fervently that they all be kept from
harm. Then she said the Lord's Prayer and the hand sank slowly
down out of sight. Uttering a prayer of thanks, she fell into a
peaceful and untroubled sleep. They stayed on at Powder Mills for

several weeks and Theo's mother never felt the evil influence near the caravan again, but did not feel easy in some places nearby and would never walk alone on that part of the moor at night.

A friend of Theo Brown called William Webb, who did like walking on the moor at night and who was not afraid of anything, was walking down the B3212 toward Postbridge one very dark night when he heard a truly appalling scream. It was not that of any animal he knew and like nothing else he had ever heard before, and for the first time in his life he was really frightened. He never found out what it was.

In 1961, forty years after the first three accidents in 1921, a car was found overturned at exactly the same spot but the driver was dead so it could never be verified whether this was the work of the hairy hands. Both car and corpse were rigorously subjected to forensic tests but no explanation of the accident was found.

Then, in 1978, a Somerset doctor turned his car onto its side at the same place, ending up in the ditch near Archerton Drive. He does not mention 'hairy hands' but, as he survived, the first-hand account of his experience is invaluable. He believed that:

> ...some malignant force had sent the car out of control. The atmosphere inside the car suddenly became deathly cold and I had a feeling almost like paralysis. I stopped the car and found I was trembling all over but I could think of no rational explanation for it. I'd had nothing to drink and, as far as I knew, I was perfectly healthy. Well, in a couple of minutes the feeling passed off and I drove on but after about two hundred yards it came back worse than ever. Although I didn't see anything specific, I was aware of a great weight or force inside the car, something quite out of my control. The steering wheel seemed to go wild and it was wrenched out of my hands. The car skidded right across the road and next second I was hanging from my seat-belt. It was terrifying and quite inexplicable and I know I didn't imagine that feeling I had before. Some people ask me if I got mildly concussed in the crash and dreamed up the whole business but I was conscious the whole time and I didn't have a single bruise.

There have not been any reported recurrences of the 'hairy hands' phenomenon since then and Theo Brown's mother thought, even in 1925, that the 'influence' was beginning to withdraw to the northern part of the moor. There have been accidents along that road as far as Merrivale but no further sightings of the hands.

Perhaps the 'hairy hands' were the manifestation of a previous accident victim at that spot, or perhaps they embodied some elemental force existing there since prehistoric times. Close to that spot, on the slopes of Lakehead Hill, there is an ancient settlement called Kraps Ring, while Bellever Forest abounds in cists, cairns, stone rows and hut circles. Perhaps the ancient spirits inhabiting this sacred, numinous area, which is more or less the centre of Dartmoor, resented the intrusion of the road and its infernal combustion engines and were expressing their displeasure at modern man's noisy, polluting invasion.

THIRTEEN

THE CANDLE OF BRIDGERULE

In the village of Bridgerule, near the market town of Holsworthy, there once lived a poor widow, as is all too often the case, who had an only daughter called Margaret. Margaret had always been a pretty child, but when she entered her teens she became more and more beautiful, which made her mother more and more worried, fearing that her beauty might bring bad luck and attract an unsuitable suitor. Moreover, the girl had been born during the chimes of midnight between a Friday and a Saturday, making her a 'Chime Child' and giving her the gift or curse of having dealings with the supernatural world. They were superstitious times in the early nineteenth century, and Margaret's mother was an ordinary countrywoman, a devout church-goer who believed in witches, pixies, the Devil himself and a myriad other uncanny perils that constantly threatened her hard, ignorant, poverty-stricken rural existence. There were so many things you must not do if you did not want to attract the evil powers, but to her mother it seemed as if Margaret was intent on doing them all.

One Sunday – it was 21 June, one of the old pagan festivals – matters between Margaret and her mother came to a head, while the very air of that close, oppressive Midsummer's Day seemed electrically charged with menace and uncertainty. Margaret was busily turning the mattress over on her bed.

'Oh my dear Lord!' cried her mother. 'Doan' 'ee knaw 'tis fearful unlucky to turn a feather bed on a Zunday?' Margaret stopped and began trimming her nails with the scissors.

'Child!' shouted her mother. 'Doan' even think of cutting your nails today. Doan' 'ee knaw the old saw: "Who on the Sabbath pares his horn, 'twere better he had ne'er been born"!'

Margaret sighed, noisily and rebelliously, and took down the Book of Common Prayer from the shelf in the little cob and thatch cottage where they kept such things – the Bible, the prayer book and the almanac. She sat down on the old settle by the fire and read the evening prayer but soon tired of that and turned to the marriage service, for that was far more exciting. She could imagine herself as a beautiful bride, dressed in a lovely white gown and she could imagine the bridegroom, a tall, dark, handsome stranger, utterly unlike the coarse, ignorant, dirty minded boys of the village. In fact, she was conjuring him up all too well in her mind's eye when…

'Margaret, dear soul!' her mother exploded. 'Doan' 'ee knaw that the maid as reads the marriage service avore her wedding-day will never get wed, except in the churchyard on her dying day!' and she snatched the book from her daughter's hand and slapped it back down on the bookshelf, almost dislodging the Bible.

'Oh mother!' cried Margaret, jumping up from the settle and stamping her foot. 'You got nothing in your head but stupid old rhymes and a pack of old wives' tales! I'm going for a walk on this Midsummer's evening – and don't tell me not to talk to strangers – I shall do as I please!'

And she flounced out of the house and walked briskly down the lane, while her distraught mother fearfully followed her to the door, calling out to her, 'Doan' 'ee go too far afield. I seen a big ol' star in the horns of the moon last night and that do betoken wild weather and uncertain times.'

'Mother, I've had enough of your folklore,' called Margaret over her shoulder, 'so I might be back before dark and I might not'. And away she strode, leaving her mother fainting in the doorway with apprehension and anxiety.

Margaret walked out along the lane to Furze in the warm, sweet, evening air, the hedges thick and fragrant with wild roses, honeysuckle and St John's Wort.

And then, by the wood at the crossroads beyond Furze, came a handsome young gentleman walking toward her. He raised his hat to her.

'Good evening, my dear', he said with a little bow. 'Do you perchance know the way to Holsworthy?'

Margaret was confused. 'Why, sir,' she said, ''tis back the way you've come. Did you not notice it?'

'I've never been in these parts before,' he said, laughing, 'but I find them very much to my taste, especially now'. And he turned and walked with Margaret down the lane toward Pyeworthy, chatting agreeably of matters of which Margaret knew nothing but was fascinated to hear – of foreign countries, modern novels and music, operas, fashion and the different customs and beliefs of different people, until Margaret's mind was whirling at a reckless speed.

At the rectory gates he stopped, saying, 'I have to leave you now, my dear Margaret, but may I meet you at the same place and at the same time tomorrow, when perhaps you could show me more of this delightful neighbourhood?'

'Willingly, sir', said Margaret, curtsying. As she watched him turn down the driveway to the rectory, she thought he must be a guest of the vicar, which must surely please her mother.

However, when she had walked back to Bridgerule in the thickening gloom, she did not tell her mother about this strange meeting but went straight to bed, to dream of her tall, dark, handsome stranger. All the next day she could think of nothing else but the evening and the young gentleman. She even looked at the new moon through the glass window of the cottage over her left shoulder to make sure it wasn't raining – a very unlucky thing to do.

At last it was time and she walked quickly to the crossroads. She walked all evening with him, listening to his exotic talk and becoming more and more enraptured with him. At the end he said he would like to spend the whole day with her on the morrow and perhaps even take her away with him to where he lived with his grandmother, whom he would very much like her to meet.

'There's nothing I'd like more,' said Margaret, 'but come and call for me at home – then you can meet my mother and 'twill all be above board'.

'Very well, Margaret,' laughed the young gentleman, 'all above board it shall be'.

But home again that night, in the darkness and solitude of her own room, doubts and fears came creeping into her head. It had all been so sudden. She had met him at Midsummer, in the twilight. He had not known where Holsworthy was, and although he said he was staying at Pyeworthy Rectory, she hadn't seen him go in. Anyway, vicars were a rum lot themselves. That there vicar of Luffincott just down the road was a queer cove, who possessed strange books and was said to dabble in dark materials unfit for a minister of the Church of England. No, she would confide in her mother tomorrow and tell her the whole story, or Lord knew what trouble might befall.

Sure enough, next day her mother didn't like the sound of her daughter's new acquaintance at all.

'Tell me quick, child,' she said, 'was he dark or fair and did you take any particular notice of his feet?'

'Can't say as I did, mother', Margaret replied. 'What ought to be wrong with 'em?'

'You got to make sure,' said her mother, 'that any stranger to the village haven't got a cloven hoof and they be a terrible hard disfigurement to hide.'

'Why should strangers have cloven hooves, mother?' asked Margaret. 'Tidn' everyone outside west Devon as do 'ave a goat for a father – though now I comes to think on it, he do wear a funny old boot on his left foot that idn' so smart as the rest of him.'

Her mother was now certain that this strange gentleman, for all his fine talk and winning ways, or perhaps because of them, was no fit suitor for her daughter; so together they went to see the parish priest. He shared the mother's fears, saying, 'Strangers are not a good thing in a country parish, especially if they are eloquent and bear a deformed foot. They are either the Devil himself or Lord Byron, and either way we must save Margaret from him'.

The priest gave Margaret's mother the stub of a church candle, with strict instructions what to do with it, and that evening it was the mother who answered the loud, peremptory knock at the door, the lighted candle in her hand.

'Is Margaret ready to come with me?' the dark gentleman asked in a low but very commanding voice. 'Or may I come in and wait until she is?'

'Er – no,' breathed the mother, shaking, 'but could you wait outside just until this little stub of a candle has burned down to nothing? Then Margaret will go with you, as she's promised.'

'Very well', said the young man. 'I'll wait until the candle is burned out.'

The mother closed the door on him with a shudder, pinched the candle out 'twixt finger and thumb, hastened quietly out through the back door and hurried to the church, where the priest met her by the altar. Together they walled up the candle in a secret recess that the priest had prepared earlier by the rood screen.

Meanwhile, Margaret was watching the stranger with a mixture of terror and desire from behind the curtains. All at once, at the very moment when the priest laid the last brick, the dark stranger disappeared in a great burst of blue flame, a sulfurous stench of rotten eggs and an enormous flash of forked lightning in the rapidly darkening sky. There was a huge roll of thunder overhead and the rain came down in torrents.

Margaret's mother breathed a deep sigh of relief as the tension broke and the air cleared but the priest said, 'Remember, if ever that candle should be taken from its niche, lit and burned down, your daughter's soul will be snatched by the Prince of Darkness, even though she lay in the very Bliss of Paradise'.

And they stood in the shelter of the church porch and watched the rain come down – and to this day that candle lies walled up in its recess behind the rood screen of Bridgerule Church, and there may it lie for all eternity.

FOURTEEN

FAIRY OINTMENT

Once upon a time there was a midwife who lived on her own in a cottage near Holne, a beautiful little village on the south-eastern slopes of Dartmoor, not far from Buckfastleigh. She was highly skilled in all the mysteries of birth and of other important matters, such as life and death. Some overly religious people called her a witch but she did not mind them, for the whole district needed her skills far more than it needed their narrow faith.

One dark and stormy night between summer and harvest, with a thunderstorm brewing over the moor, she had just snuggled down in her nice warm bed and was dropping off to sleep, when she was startled awake by a loud, insistent banging on her door. Being a midwife she was used to this, babies coming at their appointed hour and not ours, so she threw a great red cloak over her nightdress, bustled down the stairs and opened the door. To her amazement, there on a huge black horse sat a shrivelled little squint-eyed pixy in a green cloak and hood, just about to lean down and batter on her door again with his riding-crop.

'You must attend to my wife!' he shouted above the rising wind. 'She's having a baby and is like to die!'

'Are you mad?' she said, for she feared the little fellow. 'Even if the Queen of England needed me, I wouldn't go out on a night like this!' And she would have shut the door on him but...

'You'll not be harmed!' he pleaded. 'And I'll pay you well – 100 gold guineas!' That was more than the midwife earned in a year so she clambered up behind the pixy, just as she was in cloak and night-gown, for it was a warm night despite the growling of the thunder.

'For your own protection you must be blindfolded', said the pixy, tying a green silk scarf over her eyes. Then they were off and away, galloping into the dark on the rising wind, the rain coming down, the thunder rolling like cannon fire round a pitch black sky, the lightning searing the night and illuminating, for a single second, the wild, rain-ragged moor. They rode, faster and faster, far further than the midwife knew the moor stretched, outstrip-ping even the storm, until all was calm and the horse slowed and then stopped.

The pixy helped the woman down and removed her blindfold. She looked around, blinked, rubbed her eyes and looked again. She was standing in a valley she had never seen, bathed in a light she had never seen – a soft, mauve twilight, neither night nor day but luminous, making the green of the gently rolling hills quite startling and the green of the woods deeper and deeper, drawing her into their menacing depths. Swiftly, the pixy took her by the arm and led her into a humble cottage with sagging thatch and peeling walls. He led her down a dark corridor, up some narrow stairs and into a small bedroom, where a wizened little pixy wom-an lay on a bed in the throes of a terrible labour.

'Babies are rare with us now,' said the pixy, 'and a healthy baby almost unheard of. Do what you can, I beg you, but please – above all – save the mother'.

The midwife went to work with all her skill and all her will and put her heart into it as well, and some hours later a child was born, a tiny, squealing pixy child with a screwed-up face and pointed ears, hideous to behold. The pixy then gave the midwife a jar of ointment.

'Rub this into the child's eyes,' he said, 'and I'll get you your money'. While he was gone, the midwife did as she was told and rubbed some of the ointment onto the baby's eyelids. At once the ugly little creature stopped its squalling and became calm and serene. Curious, the midwife rubbed a small amount of the ointment onto her own right eyelid and then closed the left one.

To her amazement everything was transformed. The humble cottage was a fairytale castle, the pixy-woman a beautiful princess, while the baby was the loveliest child she had ever helped into the world. Just then a handsome young prince came in through the door, holding a bag of money.

At once the midwife opened her left eye and the prince became the wrinkled little pixy and she was back in the cottage again, except that a thin residue of the glamour hung over the scene still. Summoning great presence of mind, she concealed her astonishment, said nothing, and took the money.

'100 gold guineas, as promised,' said the pixy, 'and well worth every penny. Our thanks to you forever and now I'll take you home'. He led the midwife outside to where the huge black horse was waiting, quickly blindfolded her again and helped her up onto the horse. And then they were off and away again, swifter than the wind before them, outstripping the wind behind. Soon they were in the storm again, the gale tugging at the midwife's cloak, the rain lashing all around, the thunder crashing, the lightning flashing. The horse gradually slowed to a stop, the pixy helped the woman down, the blindfold was removed and she found herself outside her own cottage.

'Thank you!' shouted the pixy against the howling of the wind. 'We are in your debt forever!' and he reined the horse round and galloped off into that dark and stormy night. The midwife went wearily back to bed and the next morning, when she awoke, she wondered if it had all been a dream. But there was the bag full of guineas on the dresser. They had not turned to leaves and she counted them and bit one. They were real, like her adventure!

Then a thought struck her and she closed her left eye. The cottage was still her cottage, but it all looked grander somehow and bigger. Her cat was huge, like some heraldic beast and was without doubt of noble lineage. Her heightened senses perceived an Egyptian ancestor.

Excited, she decided to go and spend some of the money that very day at the market in Ashburton, so she hitched up the old pony and jingle and set out down the steep lanes to Buckfastleigh. As she drove along she saw that although it was a bright sunny day, as it often is after a storm, the sky was full of stars, so clear and penetrating was her sight.

At the market she closed her left eye again and here too everything was transformed. Anything beautiful was a dozen times more so, while anything ugly was unbearably hideous. Good people appeared like shining saints or angels, while bad people were beasts or demons from some painted vision of the inferno. And here and there, passing among the crowd but clearly invisible to it, were tall, noble, perfect beings in ancient dress, helping themselves to whatever they wanted from the stalls. Suddenly she saw among them the fairy prince whose wife and child she had saved.

At the same instant he saw her looking at him. Immediately he strode across to her, looking alarmed.

'With which eye do you see me?' he demanded.

'W-with the r-right eye, my lord', she stammered.

'Ah, the ointment', he muttered. 'I'm very sorry, for we owe you much, but there's nothing else to be done'. And he struck her lightly on the right eye, which was instantly blinded and when she opened her left eye there were no noble beings at all in Ashburton market – just ordinary human beings and stalls full of turnips and dishcloths. The midwife was blind in her right eye for the rest of her life and she never saw the fair folk again, but neither did she ever lack for anything, for good fortune and prosperity went with her to the end of her days.

FIFTEEN

MORE PIXY TALES

TOM WHITE

There once lived a beautiful dairymaid at Huccaby Farm on the east bank of the West Dart River above Hexworthy Bridge. She had many suitors, but the one she favoured most was young Tom White over at Postbridge. He was so in love with her he would walk the five miles from Postbridge to Huccaby after a hard day's work just to spend the evening with her and then walk back. Over Lakehead Hill he'd go, down past Bellever Tor, past Laughter Tor, then down across the open moor to Huccaby. He'd do this several times a week, summer and winter, which proved his devotion.

One midsummer's evening Tom was late and when Mary finished her work in the dairy she went up to her room to look out of her window for him, to see if he were coming down the hill behind the house. As she turned back into the room something caught her eye and, glancing back, she saw the thin crescent of a new moon just risen over the rim of the moor. Ah! But she had seen it over her left shoulder and that boded ill.

However, the evening was spent pleasantly enough, though it was much later than usual when Tom set off home. The stars were shining brightly as he toiled up past Laughter Tor toward Bellever and Tom was worried that he would not get enough sleep for his long day's work tomorrow, when he heard the sound of merry voices, music and singing from up ahead. The great granite bastions of Bellever Tor looked strangely fantastic in the moonlight, like the battlements of some otherworldly castle, and when Tom rounded a huge boulder, there on a smooth piece of level turf was a large crowd of queer small folk, all curiously dressed in green frock-coats with tall stovepipe hats, stockings and silver shoes, dancing merrily in a ring to the sawing of several fairy fiddlers.

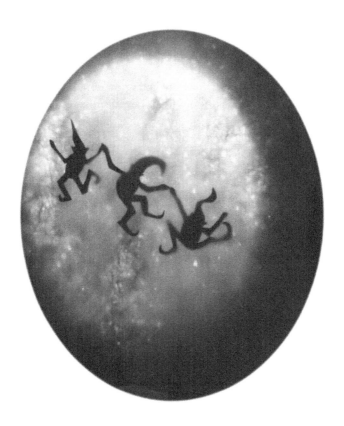

Tom was scared silly and wanted to slip away into the darkness, but the pixies had seen him and they all rushed over to him, surrounding him, grabbing his arms and leading him into the dance, shrieking with laughter and malice, glancing up askance at him with their wizened little inhuman faces and their ancient, sad eyes. He tried to get away but they held him in the dance. The music itself rooted him to the spot and made his legs jig up and down without mercy. He was terrified. He knew the stories of human beings held in the fairy world for what seemed like one night, only to be spewed out hundreds of years later. And he was tired – mortally tired – but his legs would not stop capering like a madman. At last, when he felt he really would die from exhaustion, the stars thinned, the light paled in the east and the cocks at Postbridge began to crow.

The pixies vanished into thin air and Tom fell in a faint to the ground. When he awoke it was fully light and, tired as he was, it was time to start work. He did not know how he got through that day and he earned a hard word from the farmer many a time, but when the day ended Tom swore he would never go courting to Huccaby again and he never did. He lived out his days as a bachelor and young Mary, the beautiful dairymaid of Huccaby Farm, had to find another young man to be her beau. It wasn't difficult.

JAN COO

The East and West Dart rivers meet at Dartmeet, one of the most attractive spots on the moor. Just downriver from there, where Bench Tor overlooks the wooded valley of the Dart and Blackpool, there stands on the opposite side, on the steep slopes of Sharp Tor, the isolated farm of Rowbrook. Here an orphan boy was employed as a farmhand to tend the cattle. He was a quiet lad normally and did his work well, but one winter's evening he burst into the farmhouse kitchen where the family and the farm workers were telling tales by the light of the fire and cried out, all excited, 'There be someone calling down by river. I reckon they'm in trouble'. The farmworkers left their snug, warm seats by the fire and followed the boy down the steep combe past Luckey Tor to the banks of the river, yet at first all they heard were the rushing waters of the Dart in the darkness below them. Then, quite close to them, they heard a voice calling, 'Jan Coo! Jan Coo!'

'That's my name!' said the boy. 'Where be 'ee tu? What du 'ee want?' But no reply came. Lights were brought and a thorough search of the riverbank was made, but not a trace of anyone was found.

The following night, when the men were gathered round the fire, the boy ran in from the yard again with the same tale of a voice crying in the darkness down by the river. Again they hurried down to the bank and after a short time heard the voice calling plaintively, 'Jan Coo! Jan Coo!' The men shouted in reply but all was still and silent so they went back to the warmth of the kitchen, where one of the older men said, ''Tis the piskies, I reckon'.

'Ah, you'm right', said another old chap. 'Us'd better let'n bide and not meddle with'n'.

The winter passed and the first primroses of spring were seen along the lanes. The boy Jan Coo and one of the farm workers were climbing the steep slope from the river to the farm and the dusk was closing in fast around them, when they heard the familiar voice calling to them from Langmarsh Pit on the other side of the river, 'Jan Coo! Jan Coo!' The boy shouted back, 'What du 'ee want?' but the voice went on calling, 'Jan Coo! Jan Coo!'

''Tis me they want', said the boy. 'I'll go and see who 'tis'. And he scrambled down the hill again toward the river. His companion could not stop him and watched him begin to cross the Dart on the many boulders that jumbled the riverbed. Then the dimpsy light faded and the boy was lost to sight; but still the voice called from beyond the river, 'Jan Coo! Jan Coo!' and now there was a yearning, compelling quality in its tone. The man reached the farmhouse door and had his hand on the latch when the voice stopped. He waited, listening intently, but it never came again.

The only sound breaking the stillness of the night was the murmuring of the river down below.

He went into the kitchen and told the other men what had happened and they waited for the boy to return, but he never did. They went to look for him but they never found him.

'Piskies have got him', said one of the old men. 'They'll keep him for a year and a day and when he comes back, he'll be hundreds of years old and fall to dust on the spot.'

''Twas more likely the voice of the river calling him', said another old man. 'You do all know the saying':

> River of Dart, O River of Dart
> Every year thou claim'st a heart.

And the boy was never seen again, nor was the voice heard, even on the darkest night.

CHUDLEIGH ROCKS AND OTHER SNIPPETS

Chudleigh Rocks are a large clump of limestone rocks and cliffs, honeycombed with caves; they are frequented by rock-climbers and speleologists and were popularly supposed to be a home of the pixies, one inner cave being called 'the Pixies' Parlour'. I myself have crawled through the caves from one side to the other, followed by a group of adults with learning disabilities and a French family who thought I knew what I was doing.

In Victorian times, according to Theo Brown, Chudleigh women tied their babies to their cradles to prevent them being carried away by the pixies, as was thought to have happened in another South Devon village, where all the people were of less than normal size and therefore changelings. This belief, that 'the little people' would steal human babies and substitute their own, because their own were weak and puny, was widespread, not just in Devon but throughout Europe, particularly in rural communities.

Lady Rosalind Northcote was told by a local that a gamekeeper once lived by the rocks with his wife and two small children. One morning the elder child wandered off and was lost for days, her parents looking everywhere for her, helped by all the neighbours and even a pair of bloodhounds donated by the lord of the manor. Finally she was found quite near the cottage by a couple of young men gathering nuts. She had no clothes on but was well and happy and playing with her toes. It was assumed that she had been taken by the pixies, but no one could explain why she had been returned.

We once told stories every year at a festival called Campus in Devon and late one night, around midnight, we were sitting round the campfire with a group of adults, swapping stories and singing songs. My wife Wendy had just sung the ballad 'Thomas the Rhymer', which tells of Thomas of Ercildoune's abduction into the land of the fair folk in the Middle Ages, when a woman we did not know said quietly that she had been taken away by the fairies when she was a little girl and that she had never told anyone about it until now. The hypnotic, dreamlike quality of the ballad had brought it all back to her. She had been very young, about three or four, and she had gone to sleep under a hawthorn tree. She had been missing for several days and her parents had been distracted, fearing the worst. Then she had suddenly turned up again, sitting under the same hawthorn tree, none the worse for wear. She could not remember very much about where she had been, except that it was like a palace and everyone dressed very splendidly and held a perpetual banquet, eating and drinking and listening to music and stories and dancing all the time. Certainly she had not been at all hungry after her ordeal but again you wonder what really happened to her and why she was brought back.

There are many cases of people being 'pixy led' on and around Dartmoor; of being lost, like John Fitz, for no good reason. The only cure is to turn your pockets or your coat inside out. Apart from teasing people and luring them into all-night dances, pixies could also be useful, threshing corn for farmers, sweeping the farmhouse kitchen and pinching lazy servants, provided you rewarded them with a bowl of cream. What you must not do is make new clothes for them. Then they'll be off and never help you again. But there are not many of them around these days. They have been driven underground by Christianity and the sound of church bells, which they can't abide, for they are an amoral, unchristian little race. Some people say they were once tall and noble, like the Tuatha De Danaan of Ireland, but have dwindled into 'the little people' through our lack of belief in them. I once interviewed an old quarry worker at Okehampton who was supposed to have seen them up on the moor, but he would not talk to me about it, fearing ridicule perhaps or fearing what the pixies might do to him if he blabbed about them.

SIXTEEN

THE TWO FARMERS

Once upon a time on eastern Dartmoor there lived two farmers, Farmer Oak and Farmer Ash. They were neighbours and they were wealthy. They owned much land, herds of cows, droves of horses, flocks of sheep and goats and many serfs or slaves who worked for them. Farmer Oak was kind to his serfs. He fed them well, housed them well, did not overwork them and treated them as equals. But Farmer Ash was cruel to his serfs. He starved them, kept them in hovels and whipped them. Farmer Oak was loved by his serfs and Farmer Ash was hated by his. Ash resented this so one day in autumn he said to Farmer Oak, 'Why don't you treat your serfs properly?'

'I do', said Farmer Oak.

'No you don't', said Ash. 'Serfs should be beaten and starved'.

'Why?' asked Oak.

'Well, because, um…' Ash could not think of a good reason so he burst out with, 'I bet everything I own against everything you own that I'm right and you're wrong!'

'Very well,' said Oak, 'but how do we prove it?'

'We'll ride out over the moor,' said Ash, 'and ask the first three people we meet and as they say so shall it be'.

'Very well', said Oak, though he thought to himself, 'This is silly'.

They set off at once. It was a bright, cold day and by and by they saw a young man walking briskly ahead of them, so they overtook him and reined in their horses.

'I say, fellow,' said Farmer Ash, 'we're both rich farmers and own lots of serfs. My neighbour here treats his serfs like his own family, while my serfs are beaten and starved. Who is right?'

'You're in the right', said the young man. ''Tis only natural that serfs should be beaten and starved, 'tis the way of the world, 'tis what they're for'.

'Hah! You see!' crowed Farmer Ash and on they rode. But they didn't know that the young man was a devil going about in human form, spreading lies on the face of the earth.

After a while Oak and Ash met up with a stout, middle-aged man riding a long-suffering pony. Farmer Oak asked him the question this time.

'Ah, it doesn't do to treat serfs too softly', said the man. 'They get lazy and uppity and discontented – a bit of beating and a spot of hunger keeps them on their toes'.

'Hah! You see!' gloated Farmer Ash, but it was the same devil in a different guise. On they rode and after a while they overtook an old man hobbling along with the aid of a stick. They put the question to him.

'Well,' said the old man, 'you've got to be cruel to be kind. Give your serfs a hard time in this life and they'll be rewarded in heaven. Yes! Beat them! Starve them! For all you're worth! They'll thank you in heaven'. It was the same devil and he hobbled off, chuckling to himself.

'There you are!' cried Farmer Ash. 'And here I am! And I've won everything you own!' Farmer Oak got down from his horse and handed the reins to Farmer Ash.

'Yes,' he said sadly, 'everything I once possessed is now yours, except my wife and children. Tell my wife I'm going to look for work and I'm not coming back 'till I've regained all that I've lost by this stupid bet'.

'It'll be a long time before she sees you again, then!' sneered Farmer Ash as he reined his horse round and, leading Oak's horse, rode back the way they'd come.

Farmer Oak walked on deeper and deeper into the moor, up over Shovel Down, past the old Long Stone and the Stone Rows, then down along past Teignhead Farm and Quintin's Man, meaning to make it to the other side of the moor where he would not be known. As he walked the country became wilder, bleaker, more and more desolate; the rain started to come down and the day began to thicken into night. Just before it was pitch dark he came to a great tor of piled, jumbled rocks and at the foot of it an empty, tumbledown house – an old tinner's hut. He went in and though there was only one room and no roof, there was a big chimney place at one end that was comparatively dry.

Farmer Oak huddled down on the damp stones and tried to go to sleep. He was just dropping off when he heard a trampling of hooves and a flapping of leathery wings, a whooping and a screeching and he just had time to scramble up the chimney before a host of devils burst in. This was the place they met each night to report on all the mischief they'd done during the day. Farmer Oak was terrified but he braced himself against the old iron bar from which the kettle dangled and hung on for his life. The devils were making one hell of a noise boasting about all the evil they'd done and Farmer Oak could not hear a word, when the Demon King bellowed, 'Silence! Is this a devils' meeting or *Yesterday in Parliament*?' Then the devils were ashamed and each one spoke in turn, while Farmer Oak listened intently to everything they said.

First an ugly devil with a long beak and bat's wings told of the lies he'd spread, diddling a good farmer out of everything he owned. ('Did you so?' murmured Oak, but stayed where he was.)

Then a tall, dry devil made of baked clay said, 'I've done better than that. To the north of the moor lies a town, once known as the Rich Town, for a magical stream ran through it which bestowed health and good fortune; but I have stopped it with a granite boulder jammed into the spring and the town will soon be known as the Poor Town'.

There was wild applause and sniggering admiration, and the Demon King chortled, 'Good! Good! But is the mischief safe? Is there no way it can be undone?'

'Well,' drawled the dry devil, 'our power is limited, as you know. If a man were to take a virgin sword and strike the boulder to north, south, east and west and say, "Boulder, begone!" then the boulder would jump out and the stream would flow – but who on earth would think of that?'

'No one!' roared the Demon King, and the devils hooted and stamped and farted and spat.

'I've done better than that!' screeched a mad devil with teeth like Ken Dodd's. 'To the south of the moor lies a city ruled by a king, who has one daughter who is the darling of the city. I sat on her bed last night, talking quietly to her and showing her… things, and now she is staring mad and squats on her pillow, gibbering. The doctors cannot cure her, the king is mad with grief and the whole city is in despair'.

'Splendid!' rumbled the Demon King. 'But can the spell be undone?'

'Well,' sneered the mad devil, 'our power is limited – Bleugh! If someone sat up with the princess all night, talking about nice things – Bleugh! Feugh! Schpleugh! – then led her to the window just before dawn so that the first ray of the rising sun struck her forehead, she would be cured. But who would think of that? Wollicum snoggerlumps!'

'No one!' roared the Demon King, and the devils cackled and capered and got out their lava pipes and smoked their Sinner's Soul & Brimstone tobacco. The fumes rose up the chimney and clouded Farmer Oak's brain so that he fell asleep, though he still hung on to his precarious perch. And when he came to, it was a cold, grey morning and the devils had departed. He clambered down, muttering, 'That was a horrible dream!' but then he saw the cloven hoofprints on the trampled mud floor, while the air was still laced with a tang of infernal tobacco and he knew it had been real.

'Well,' he said to himself, 'now to see if devils speak the truth!' And away he went, northward across the moor, over tors, over bogs, over streams and across the great heather-clad shoulders of the hills, until he came to the north of the moor where lay the town now known as the Poor Town.

It was in a sorry state. The cattle were thin, the crops were dying and the people slouched about with long faces, as if they'd received a death sentence. Farmer Oak went to see the mayor, who readily agreed to anything Oak suggested. They went straight to the blacksmith who made a brand new sword there and then. Armed with this, Farmer Oak followed the empty stream bed up to its source on the high moor and there, couched in a marshy hollow, lay a great granite boulder of a sinister aspect, being perfectly round and smooth, though covered in lichen. A fearful aura of menace and danger pervaded the place but Oak gripped the sword and descended into the hollow. The stone towered above him, exuding malevolence, but he wielded the sword, striking the boulder on its northern side. Then he shuffled round and struck it on its eastern side, then to the south and lastly to the west. Finally he backed up out of the hollow and said the words, 'Boulder, begone!'

Immediately he hurled himself to the ground, for the huge boulder hurtled up out of the hollow with a force that would have taken his head off and went rolling away over the moor. The pent-up stream leapt out of the ground into its old bed and ran down toward the town faster than Oak could keep up with it.

When he got to the town the stream was chattering happily through it once more and people and animals were lining its banks, drinking greedily, while the irrigation ditches carried the precious water to the fields.

'We can never repay you enough!' cried the mayor and the whole town agreed that Farmer Oak deserved half of everything they possessed. So he became a rich man again and a caravan of cattle, horses and sheep, and wagons full of goods and serfs set out for his home on the eastern side of the moor, while Oak himself, mounted on a fine black stallion, rode south.

All that day he rode, over tors, over bogs, over streams and across the great heather-clad shoulders of the hills, until he came to the city on the southern side, a mighty, bustling seaport. As he rode in through the gates, he noticed all the people going about in black with mournful faces and he went straight to see the king. The king was in despair and clutching at straws so he readily agreed to let Farmer Oak try his luck.

All that night Oak sat up with the princess, talking to her calmly and patiently, while she crouched on her pillow, gibbering and muttering and staring wildly round the room. He talked of the things he knew best, ordinary things such as the plants and the animals, the seasons, the stars and the sun, and gradually she grew calmer. Then, just before dawn, he led her gently to the window and, as the sun rose above the low, eastern hills, the first of its rays touched her forehead and her face cleared, the demon departed from her and her reason returned. The king was overjoyed and the whole city agreed that Farmer Oak deserved half of everything they possessed, and Oak became a hundred times richer than he had been before.

He set out for his home on the eastern side of the moor with a vast caravan of animals, wagons and men and when he arrived, there waiting for him was the caravan from the Rich Town. His wife and family were overjoyed to see him again but Farmer Ash was furious.

'Where the hell did you get all this from?' he roared and Farmer Oak, being honest, told him all about the tumbledown house and the devils' confabulation, the Rich Town and the king's daughter. Farmer Ash immediately mounted his horse and rode off into the moor, determined to try his luck as well, in spite of Farmer Oak's warnings.

It was already getting dark when Ash arrived at the tumble-down house under Fur Tor so, tying his horse to a gorse stump on the other side of the tor, he crept into the ruin and hid up the chimney. Soon a great trampling of hooves and a leathery flapping of wings, a screeching and a cackling announced the arrival of the devils. But they were in a fearful temper, for all the mischief they had done had been undone and all their evil had been made good. The devils were in a dreadful hullabaloo about it, until the Demon king roared, 'Silence! Is this a devils' meeting or a conference of storytellers? There's only one answer! We have a spy! An eavesdropper! Seek him out!'

There was only one place to hide in that ruin so scaly arms reached up the chimney and sharp talons dug into Farmer Ash's flesh and dragged him down onto the mud floor, where the devils surrounded him and blew on him with their searing breath. Ash, writhing in agony, shrunk and dwindled until he was nothing at all and that was the end of him; but Farmer Oak took over both farms and treated Ash's serfs as well as his own and lived out his days in happiness and prosperity.

SEVENTEEN

THE THREE SILLIES

This is a reconstruction of a well-known English folk tale that I found once in a Devonshire dialect version in the Westcountry Studies Library in Exeter. It had been printed in Ilfracombe in 1922. I came across it about twenty years ago at the beginning of my career as a storyteller and I have not found it since then. It is like the lost chord. If anyone knows where I can find a copy of it, I would be grateful.

In the county of Devonshire, in the parish of Idiotesleigh, at Dumb Bunny Farm, there once lived a farmer called Farmer Nincompoopacott, with his wife, Mrs Nincompoopacott, and their daughter, Mary-Jane Nincompoopacott. Mary-Jane was the prettiest maid for miles around and a strapping lass for the housework she was, for she never begrudged plenty of elbow-grease. 'Course, she soon had plenty of young men sighing after her, but she had eyes for only one and that was young Tom Chidleycott, the red-headed plough-boy on the next farm.

Every Sunday young Tom'd come courting and in they days that meant he'd sit up one end of a table, Mary-Jane'd sit down t'other end and Mr and Mrs Nincompoopacott would sit in the middle, to make sure there was no hanky-panky. But there'd be a great fruitcake on the table and a great jug of Wobble-brain cider and all the juiciest village gossip they could chew on, like who the vicar was seeing to these days and a rare old time would be had by all.

So one Sunday afternoon they were all sitting there as usual, gossiping and guzzling and glolloping down cake, when all at once the cider ran out and Mary-Jane, being a willing girl, took the jug down the cellar to fill it up again. She put the jug under the big barrel of cider in the corner, turned on the tap and, while waiting for the jug to fill, glanced idly around the cellar. Her eye chanced to alight on a great iron hammer balanced precariously on a wooden beam just above her head and, being an imaginative sort of girl, she got to thinking:

> Yer, s'pose me and Tom was to get married and s'pose we was to have a little bway and s'pose he was to come down here to get cider, just like what I be a-doing, and s'pose thick gurt 'ammer was to fall down on his head and kill 'en stone dead? Wouldn't that be terrible? Oh dear, oh dear, oh Lord!

And there and then she plumped down on the cellar floor and started crying her eyes out, fit to burst, pulling her skirts and petticoats over her head and rocking to and fro. And the cider overflowed the jug and went swimming all over the floor.

By and by, those in the kitchen began to wonder what was keeping her, so Mrs Nincompoopacott went along the passageway to the cellar door, opened it and went down the cellar steps. And there was Mary-Jane sitting on the cellar floor, skirts over her head, rocking to and fro, fit to bust.

'Lord above, maid!' said Mrs Nincompoopacott. 'Whatever's the matter with 'ee?'

Mary-Jane cried:

> Aw, mother! A terrible thing come into my head. S'pose me and Tom was married; and s'pose us was to have a little bway, and s'pose he

was to come down here to get cider; and s'pose thick gurt hammer on the beam was to come down on his head and kill 'en stone dead? Wouldn't that be a terrible thing? Boo-hoo-hoo-hoo-hoo!

Her mother said:

Well, Mary-Jane! Of all the gurt sillies – If thee doesn't beat the lot! Just s'pose you was married and s'pose you did 'ave a little bway and s'pose thick hammer did fall on his head and kill 'en – stone dead – well, 'twould be a terrible thing – terrible – poor little bway, with his brains splashed all over the cellar floor – oh, boo-hoo-hoo-hoo-hoo-hoo-hoo!

And she sat down by Mary-Jane, pulled her skirts and petticoats over her head and rocked to and fro, sobbing fit to burst. And the cider covered the cellar floor and lapped gently around their bottoms.

Up in the kitchen, Farmer Nincompoopacott and young Tom Chidleycott were wondering what was keeping the cider, so Farmer Nincompoopacott went down into the cellar. And there was Mary-Jane and her mother sitting side-be-side, rocking to and fro, sobbing fit to burst, with their skirts and petticoats pulled over their heads in a great puddle of cider.

"Ello,' says Farmer, 'be I in my own house or bain't I? What little game's going on yer, then? Is this what they d' call a panty-mime?'

'Aw, mother!' sobs Mary-Jane. 'You tell 'im. I abm' got the gumption'.

So Mrs Nincompoopacott says:

Well, s'pose Mary-Jane and young Tom was to get married an' s'pose they was to have a little bway an' s'pose he was to come down 'ere an' get cider an' s'pose thick gurt 'ammer up there was to fall down on his head an' kill 'en stone dead – wouldn' that be a terrible thing? Oh, boo-hoo-hoo-hoo-hoo-hoo-hoo!

Farmer Nincompoopacott cries:

Well, slap me girdle! Git out wi' yer cakey ol' nonsense! I never zeed sich a pair of sillies with your s'posin' this an' s'posin' that. Why, Tom hasn't even axed the maid yet! Hah! Well, s'pose they was married an' s'pose they was to 'ave a little bway an' s'pose he did come down 'ere to get cider an' s'pose thick there hammer did fall on his head an' kill 'en – stone daid! Well, there – 'twould be a terrible thing, 'twouldn' it? For me own little grandson to be killed by me own 'ammer – with all his brains squidged out down through his nose – oh, boo-hoo-hoo-hoo-hoo-hoo-hoo!

And Farmer Nincompoopacott sat right down by the other two Nincompoopacotts, stuffed his head down the top of his trousers and rocked to and fro, sobbing fit to burst and the lake of cider gradually crept up around their ample Devonshire middles.

Meanwhile, up in the kitchen, young Tom began to wonder if the cellar had one of they there black holes in it, so down the cellar steps he went and there were the three of them, rocking to and fro, sobbing fit to burst, cider up to their armpits.

'Whatever's this?' cried Tom. 'Is it a 'zylum for the inzane I be come to or is it a revivalist meeting or what?'

'Aw, mother!' sobs Mary-Jane, 'You tell 'im!'

'Aw, father!' sobs Mother, 'You tell 'im!'

'Aw, Tom!' sobs Father: 'You…':

Well, s'pose you and Mary-Jane was married an' s'pose you was to 'ave a little bway an' s'pose he was to come down 'ere to get cider an' s'pose thick there hammer should fall on his head an' kill 'en stone dead, with his skull all smashed to smithareens and his brains coming out of his eyes – wouldn't it be terrible? Oh, boo-hoo-hoo-hoo-hoo-hoo-hoo!

And Tom cries:

Well, if you three ain't the biggest sillies as I've ever come across in all my born days, I'll never go to baid more! Gaw! S'pose us was married! Purty vorrard I call that! Why, I abm' even axed the maid yet! Yer, I'll tell 'ee what – rather than marry into such a fambly of fules, I'm off an' 'ceps I find three bigger sillies than you, which idn' likely – I'll never darken your door again!

And off he went, slamming the door behind him and the three Nincompoopacotts set to sobbing worse than ever, for they thought they'd lost him and the cider crept up to their chins.

So we'll leave them there to sink or swim and follow young Tom as he leaped on his horse and rode away in a fury; but after a bit he calmed down and got to thinking what a fine, strapping maid Mary-Jane was – prettiest girl 'twixt Idiotesleigh and Monkeytown – but it was the thought of her elbow-grease that swayed him, so he thought as how he'd keep his eyes peeled to see what fools there might be going about, and if he found three bigger sillies than the Nincompoopacotts he'd go back and marry the girl.

After a bit he was riding through a farmyard and there he saw a boy, a ragged, dirty, little urchin, pouring boiling water from an old kettle into a zinc trough.

'What be 'ee doin' that vor?' he says to the boy.

'Well,' says the boy, 'I'm givin' the hens boilin' water to make 'em lay boiled eggs'.

'Get out, you gurt silly!' says Tom. 'You'll scald their insides out through their backsides. You'm a bigger silly than Mary-Jane!' and he rode on his way to a mad cackling of scalded hen.

By and by he came to a thatched cottage that had grass and dandelions growing on the roof and an old woman was trying to get her cow to climb a ladder onto the roof so it could eat the grass.

'Why doan' 'ee cut the grass,' says Tom, 'and chuck it down to the cow?'

'Oooh, 'tis too much trouble', says the old woman. 'Besides, the cow'll be quite safe. I shall tie a rope round her neck and pass it down the chimbly and tie it to me ankle. I shall soon know if zummat happens to her'.

'You certainly will,' says Tom, 'and you'm a bigger silly than Mary-Jane and her mother put together'. And he rode on his way and the cow tumbled off the roof and dangled by the wall of the cottage and strangled and the old woman was dragged up the chimney, stuck fast halfway up and was suffocated in the soot.

But Tom just rode on and that night he stayed at an inn that was so full he had to share a room of two beds with another traveller. The next morning Tom was woken by a strange noise – Guppity-guppity-guppity-guppity-waaaah! Bump! Guppity-guppity-guppity-guppity-waah! Bump! So he peeped over the bedclothes and saw that his roommate had hung his trousers on the knobs of the chest of drawers and was then running the whole length of the room and trying to jump into them – backwards – but getting his feet caught in them and landing with a thump on the floor! Tom watched him try this manoeuvre forty-nine times, until his companion stopped and wiped his face with a handkerchief and said, 'Whew! Oh dear, I do think trousers are the awkwardest clothes ever invented. It takes me an hour or two to get into mine every morning and I get so hot! Sometimes I don't manage it at all and have to go back to bed'.

'Get out, you gurt silly!' says Tom. 'Why doan' 'ee put in one foot to a time'. And he demonstrated the operation with his own pair of trousers.

'I never thought of that', says the chap.

'And you,' says Tom, 'are a bigger silly than Mary-Jane and her mother and father put together'.

So off he went, back to Dumb Bunny Farm, where he made it up with Mary-Jane and married her and, sure enough, they did have a little boy – in fact they had several little boys, and several little maids too.

Well, the story got around, as stories do, and one day the farmer Tom worked for said to him, 'Well, Tom, I s'pose the first thing you did when you had the first babby was to take down that hammer from that beam'.

'No, maister,' says Tom. 'I didn't.'

'You didn't?' says master. 'What'd 'ee do then?'

'Well,' says Tom, 'I entered all the boys in the Burial Club and trusted in Providence'.

EIGHTEEN

THE PARSON AND THE CLERK

A Bishop of Exeter lay dying and a parson of Dawlish was consumed by the ambition to become the next bishop. So, accompanied by his parish clerk, the parson set out to Exeter to visit the bishop; to ask after his condition, to comfort and tend the old man as well as he could, and to admire Exeter Cathedral, which was to be such an enviable part of his future see.

After a stay of several days, during which he fawned, curried and insinuated, the parson was assured by the ailing bishop that his attentiveness would be duly rewarded, and he set off with his clerk from Exeter's West Gate, shortly to turn south and begin the long climb up Haldon Hill.

But as their horses toiled up the thickly forested slopes, a great storm blew up and the rain came down and in the sudden darkness that descended on Haldon Forest they lost their way and were soon wandering hopelessly on small, overgrown tracks. Frightened and angry, the parson blamed his clerk.

'Curse these wretched hills and curse you!' cried the parson. 'How on earth did you manage to lose the way, you damn fool? I'd rather have the Devil as a guide than you!' Soon after this a man caught up with them, riding out of the gloom behind them, making his way confidently through the lashing wind and pouring rain.

'May I be of assistance?' he shouted against the roaring gale.

'Aye, you may!' bawled the parson. 'We're lost and must get to Dawlish before dark!'

'Then I'm going the same way as you!' shouted the man, who wore a thick, black, hooded cloak. 'I can even give you food and shelter, for my house is not far from here'. And they followed the stranger through the dark, howling wood until they came to a solitary house within sight of the sea. It was a mansion, whose windows were ablaze with welcoming lights. Servants took their horses and the stranger led them inside, where a riotous party was in full swing. The tables were groaning with food and drink and the revellers, both men and women, were noisy, shrill, lewd and blasphemous. But the warmth and the shelter from wind and rain were like Heaven to the wet, cold, miserable clerics and soon they entered into the spirit of the party, eating and drinking their fill – especially drinking – and joining in with the lewd jests and singing the blasphemous songs along with the worst of that riotous crew. Indeed, the parson's songs and jests were as foul and low-minded as any, and were greeted with cheers and coarse, uncouth approbation by that ungodly company.

The clerk, who wasn't drinking half as much as the parson, had just begun to notice that some of the partygoers were men and women long supposed to be dead, when a messenger came to the door with the news that the Bishop of Exeter had died that day.

'We'd best be going, sir', whispered the clerk to the parson. 'I fear we have tarried here too long'.

'Aye, aye!' roared the parson. 'The bloody bishop dead? Why, we must back to Exeter, man! Bid them bring the horses!'

Their horses were brought round to the front of the house and the entire company gathered at the door to see them off. The storm still raged along the coast and the darkness was now almost palpable, but the parson's ambition overwhelmed his good sense and he urged his horse on, but the beast wouldn't move. The more the two men whipped and spurred the poor horses, the more they dug their hooves in and the more the company laughed

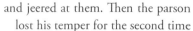

and jeered at them. Then the parson lost his temper for the second time that day and cried out, 'The Devil take the brutes!'

'Thank you, I shall!' called their host and, looking round, the parson and the clerk saw, to their horror, that he was the Devil himself, while the guests had become shrieking spectres, dead souls wailing in torment and dreadful demons. One of them lashed the horses' rumps with his forked tail and straightaway they sprang into a gallop and made for the edge of the cliff, over which they plunged, neighing wildly, the screams of the two men lost in the howling storm. Behind them the great mansion vanished with an awful lamentation of damned souls as they were driven and herded back down to hell.

Next morning the people of Dawlish talked with awe of the night's terrible storm and of strange cries and a thunder of galloping hooves that were heard above it. Two exhausted horses were found wandering quietly along Dawlish Sands, while standing in the sea, close to the cliffs, were two great sandstone rocks that had not been there before. One was much bigger than the other and to this day those two rocks are known as the Parson and the Clerk.

NINETEEN

TOM TAW

One fine, hot, summer's day, young Tom Taw went down to the big brown river to fish. He bore his fishing rod over his shoulder and in his left hand he carried his fishing basket, in which he kept his sandwiches and his worms – but not in the same container.

As he tramped along the riverbank, the hot sun beat down on his head and the sweat stood out on his brow and trickled uncomfortably down his neck. His footsteps trudged slower and slower, until they stopped and, shading his eyes, he squinted up at the bright sun and said, 'Gor blimey, Mr Sun, you'm strong today!'

And the sun beamed down at him and said, 'Yes, Tom Taw, I am strong today!' And Tom Taw mopped his brow and thought for a bit and said, 'Well, strong you may be, Mr Sun, but I know someone stronger than you':

She's so light and fluffy,
She's nearly not all there
But when she floats across the sky,
She doesn't even need to try,
She makes you disappear.

And at that moment a great dark cloud passed slowly across the face of the sun, blotting him out completely; and the cloud began to rain large, cold drops, the air got a lot cooler and Tom Taw began to shiver. And he raised his wet face to the cloud and said, 'Cor, Mrs Cloud, you'm strong! You've drove the sun away, you 'ave!'

And the Cloud frowned down at him and whispered, 'Yes, Tom Taw, I am very strong today'. And Tom shook the water from his hair and thought for a bit and said, 'Strong you may be, Mrs Cloud, but I know someone stronger than you':

> He's so light, he's hardly there at all;
> He's lighter than the whisper of a gnat's footfall.
> You can't even see him,
> Though you feel him and you hear him
> And he's so strong, he doesn't need to try
> But he can blow you, Mrs Cloud, right out of the sky.

And at that moment a great wind rose out of the west and blew and blew and blew that cloud into tatters, into thin wisps of dissolving vapour. And the wind blew stronger still and ruffled Tom Taw's hair and nearly blew the man down. But Tom steadied himself against a handy willow tree growing on the riverbank and squinnied into the eye of the wind and said, 'Gor blimey, Mr Wind, you'm strong today!' And the wind whistled into his face and said, 'Yesss, Tom Taw, I am strong today!' And Tom Taw turned his back on the wind and leaned into it and thought for a bit and said, 'Strong you may be, Mr Wind, but I know someone stronger than you':

> She's made of earth and fixed to earth,
> By huge pressures brought to birth.
> She's steep and clothed in trees and grass
> And you cannot move her mighty mass.

And the wind rushed headlong into a great hill at the source of the river and he blew against the hill; and he blew and he blew with all his strength but he couldn't budge the hill by one inch. So he blew himself out and went off in a huff.

And Tom Taw looked up at the hill and said, 'Cor, Mrs Hill, ma'am, you'm master strong!'

And the hill gazed down at him in stony silence for a while and then said, 'Tom Taw, I'm about as strong as it gets'.

And Tom Taw stared at the hill and thought for a bit and said, 'H'm, strong you may be, Mrs Hill, but I know someone stronger than you':

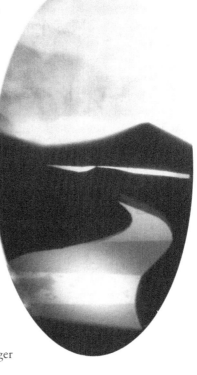

> Now they're very, very small,
> Weigh hardly anything at all
> But there's millions of them in the cloud
> And though you stand so steep and proud,
> They fall down on you, Mrs Hill
> And seep inside you, deep, until
> They delve great caves, in which they make
> A vast, unseen and sunless lake.

And a great dark cloud hung over the hill and released its drifting swathes of falling rain. And the raindrops fell on the flanks of the hill and sank down inside her until they reached her great clay heart, where they formed a network of underground pools and lakes.

But even then the hill could not keep them in her dark stone prison, for they burst out through her walls in a dozen different escapes and ran happily down her slopes, twisting, turning, dancing, sparkling – always running downward – joining each other to form one being, questing always down toward its ancient mother and now we call this being something else.

And Tom Taw ran along the bank of this big brown river and cried, 'Old Man River, you'm jolly strong. you are!' And the River swirled and eddied and sang:

> Yes, Tom Taw, I am very, very strong
> And I just keep rolling along and along.

And Tom Taw thought for a bit and laughed and said, 'Strong you may be, Old Man River, but I know someone stronger than you':

> She's waiting there to get you,
> Vast and green and blue
> And when you run right into her,
> That'll be the end of you!

And Tom Taw ran down to the lip of land where the river is devoured by the sea and he looked out over the glittering, rolling, heaving mass of salt water that covers nearly three quarters of the globe, and he called out, 'Ahoy there, Mrs Sea, you'm the strongest of the lot, it seems!'

And the sea danced and dazzled and said, 'Yes, Tom Taw, I am the strongest being on the face of this earth'. But Tom Taw thought for a bit and grinned and said, 'Strong you may be, Mrs Sea, but I know someone stronger than you':

> He's not of this earth but stands very high
> And he can suck you up into the sky,

Rob you of your salt and stop you being proud
By turning you into an insubstantial cloud.

And the sea laughed a deep, throaty chuckle and said:

And why, Tom Taw, should I want to stop the sun doing that? It's all part of the cycle, all part of the fun. That way I get to be a cloud again, a raindrop, an underground lake, a spring, a stream, a river and I get to see the fields and the woods and the hills again – and I get to provide you with fish, Tom Taw, so you be about your business and let me be about mine!

And Tom Taw bowed to Old Mother Sea and tipped his hat to Old Father Sun and went back up the bank of the big brown river to catch a nice fat fish for his tea.

TWENTY

MORE TALES OF THE TAW

THE DEVIL COMES TO BELSTONE

A Belstone sheep farmer was making a late round of his flock one bitterly cold winter's evening. Coming back by Taw Marsh in the dusk, he saw a huge pair of horns rising above the riverbank. Terrified, he took to his heels and didn't stop until he got back to Belstone, where he burst into the Tors Hotel and told everyone there that the Devil – Old Dewer himself – was lurking in Taw Marsh, planning to take over the village in the night. All that night the people of Belstone trembled with terror, unable to sleep a wink, and in the morning, after nothing had happened, a posse of stalwarts armed with pitchforks made their way fearfully up the banks of the Taw. And there in Taw Marsh they found a great red stag, frozen to death in the ice at the edge of the river. Mind you, they do say that the Devil died of the cold in Northlew, but that is surely wishful thinking. He is evidently alive and well and doing good business with the politicians.

THE TALKING HARE

This story was told by an old native of Belstone in the early 1960s. His father and one of his friends were walking home one evening across Belstone Common above Taw Marsh, carrying a young hare they had snared in a net. Suddenly a raven flew perilously low over heir heads, as if it were attacking them, and a loud voice called from the direction of Cosdon Beacon, 'Jacko! Jacko!' The little hare jumped up in the net and said, 'That's my dad calling me!' Both men were so frightened, they dropped the net, hare and all and ran for home. Next day they went back and got the net but the hare was gone. Ruth St Leger-Gordon said she could make neither head nor tail of this story and neither can I.

THE SEVEN PREBENDS OF CHULMLEIGH

The River Taw rises on Dartmoor close to Cranmere Pool, then flows down past Taw Marsh toward Belstone and through the beautiful gorge of Belstone Cleave. It flows through Sticklepath, where it powers the wheels of Finch's Foundry, then north, passing fairly close to the old manor house of the Oxenhams to North Tawton, where you can find de Bathe Pool. The Taw continues north to Nymet Rowland, home of the North Devon Savages, where it turns north-west and heads up past Eggesford and Chulmleigh on its way to Barnstaple Bay and the sea. At Chulmleigh there is another strange little story, taken from Sir Thomas Westcote's *View of Devon* (1630).

A poor man of Chulmleigh, having too many children (and knowing nothing of birth control), went away from his wife and home for seven years in the hope of stemming the flood of babies, at least for a while. But nine months after he returned, to the very day, his wife bore him seven sons all at once (poor woman!). They kept this prodigious birth secret and the poor man put his seven sons into a large basket and took them down to the River Taw, resolving to let them sink or swim, just as it pleased them.

On the way down the hill to the river he was unfortunate enough to meet the Countess of Devonshire, out doing pious works. Now this Countess was Isabella Courtenay of Powderham Castle and she possessed large estates at Tiverton and Chulmleigh. It was said of her that she planted the oaks of Wistman's Wood on Dartmoor, and she was an extremely pious and religious woman. Meeting a poor man struggling down the hill from Chulmleigh toward the River Taw, bearing a large basket from which a curious mewling emanated, she became divinely inspired and demanded to know what was in it.

'Whelps, if you please, ma'am,' mumbled the poor fellow, 'blind puppies not worth the rearing.'

'Let me see 'em', quoth the countess; and the more he was loath, the more she was determined and so the poor man, realising that the only way to get rid of the old busybody was to drown her too – which would have been a dreadful bother – at last fell on his knees, opened the basket and showed her the brats, confessing his intention toward them.

The good Countess Isabella took them home with her and provided them with wet nurses. She brought them up herself and gave them an education. When they were grown to man's estate, she gave each of them a prebendary in the parishes, providing for these out of the proceeds of her estates at Tiverton and Chulmleigh. The seven crosses near Tiverton are said to commemorate the occasion and it was said that it was the only time that seven neighbouring clerics agreed with one another in the two parishes.

FRANCIMASS

Also from the Taw Valley, in the beautiful countryside around Eggesford, Chulmleigh, Chawleigh and Burrington, comes a curious tradition collected in 1894 from the local people by the

Revd Sabine Baring-Gould, author of 'Onward, Christian Soldiers', a number of 'folk songs' and a clutch of sensational novels. This tradition maintains that the 19-21 May is known in this area as Francimass, or St Frankin's Days. It is a time when apple-growers and cider-makers must be on their guard, for an unseasonal frost may well descend during these days and blight the apple-blossom.

Apparently, a brewer called Frankin vowed his soul to the Devil if the Old One would send three frosty nights in May to kill off the apple blossom and ruin the cider trade. In another version, the brewer was St Dunstan. In yet another version all the brewers of beer in North Devon, lamenting the fact that everyone drank cider, got together and promised the Devil, who in this instance was called St Frankin, that they would all put nasty matter (whatever that was!) into their beer on those three days, provided the Devil frosted the apple trees then. So watch out! If there is a frost between the 19-21 May, the brewers are putting nasty matter into their beer, so I should stick to cider anyway!

JACK THE WHITE-HAT

The River Taw meanders north-west from Chulmleigh, past Chittlehamholt (with the accent on the 'holt'), Umberleigh and Bishop's Tawton to Barnstaple, flowing at last into the Atlantic Ocean in Barnstaple or Bideford Bay, depending on which town you come from. And here is the strangest story of all, a weird haunting on the southern tip of Braunton Burrows in the estuary of the River Taw, on a narrow spit of sand called 'the Neck' which ends in Crow Point. Here was seen the sinister figure of Jack the White-Hat. He could be seen from a great distance, on account of the great white hat he wore, which had a lighted lantern attached to the crown, and he would wander around on Crow Point hailing the ferry from Appledore or any other boat heading to Barnstaple.

But if any boat stopped to give him a lift, the crew would find no one there; he would have vanished, and from that time on that boat and its crew would suffer dreadfully bad luck. So everyone became terrified of 'Old White-Hat', as he was also known. It was bad luck even to see him. One story about him said he was the spirit of a miller who was doomed to this ill-omened haunting because the Devil had helped him understand and work his machinery. Theo Brown says he was a real man and has descendants living in Bideford. She also says he could have been a folk memory of the old wrecker's ploy of tying a lantern to a horse's head and leading it along the shore, to make ships coming in to the estuary think they had plenty of sea-room. It could also be a smuggler's trick to frighten people away from that part of the estuary when contraband was being landed.

We were performing 'Tales of the Taw' in Barnstaple Museum not long ago and I told this story. A young woman in the audience approached us afterward and said we had solved a childhood mystery for her. Her father had been a bargee on the Taw, plying his trade between Barnstaple and Bideford. There was one point on the estuary that scared him silly, that he wouldn't look at or even talk about, because it meant bad luck and now she knew why.

TWENTY ONE

THE FISH AND THE RING

In the county of Devonshire, during the reign of the first Queen Elizabeth, there once lived an earl whose manor house overlooked the valley of the River Taw. This earl was a magician and could read the future; so when his wife gave birth to a baby boy, he cast his son's horoscope to discover his fate and he found, to his horror, that his son was destined to marry a peasant girl who had just been born to a poor farm labourer's wife on his land.

He called for his horse and rode down to the cottage where the poor man lived, and there he found the man sitting on his door-step, his head in his hands, despairing. The earl dismounted, went up to him and said, 'What's the matter, my good man?'

'Fact is, your Lordship,' said the man, 'I've got nine children already and I'm blessed if I know where they come from and now us've got a tenth, a little maid, and I'm darned if I know how to feed 'em all'.

'Don't be downhearted, my good man,' said the earl in his most kindly voice, 'for I am here to help you. If you give me the little maid that's just been born, I'll take care of her and you needn't trouble your head about her any more'.

'Oh, thank you, sir', said the man and he went into the hovel. Despite the feeble protests of the mother, he brought out the baby girl, all in her swaddling clothes, and gave her to the earl who mounted his horse and rode away with the precious little bundle. And as he rode along the bank of the River Taw, he threw the bundle into the dark, swirling water and rode back to his manor house a contented man.

But the little maid didn't sink. Her clothes and her guardian angel kept her afloat and she drifted down the river until she fetched ashore by the hut of a fisherman. The fisherman found her and took her into his hut with joy in his heart, for he and his wife were childless and she lived with them until she was fifteen years old – and a lovely young girl she was.

One day the earl and his companions went otter-hunting along the banks of the Taw and they stopped at the fisherman's hut to get a drink of water. The girl came out with a jug and they were all struck dumb by her beauty, and one of them said to the earl, 'You can see the future William. Who will have the great good fortune to marry her?'

'Oh, some local yokel, I expect,' said the earl, 'but come here, girl, and tell me when you were born, if you can'.

'I don't really know, sir', said the girl. 'My parents say I was brought to them as a gift of the river fifteen years ago'. Then the earl knew exactly who she was, and the next day he rode back to

the hut and said to the girl, 'Listen, my dear, your fate interests me. Take this letter to my brother in Barnstaple and you will be settled for life'. The girl took the letter and when the earl had ridden away, she asked her parents what she should do. They told her to go first to her aunt, who had a small inn at Bishop's Tawton, stay there the night and then go on to the earl's brother's house in the morning, for the letter was surely an introduction for her to enter into service with the earl's brother and it would be a big step up for her.

The girl set out at once and reached her aunt's inn at Bishop's Tawton by the evening. That night, a gang of robbers broke into the inn and robbed everyone who was staying there; but the girl had no money, only the letter, so they opened it and read:

Dear Humphrey,
Take the bearer of this letter and put her to death immediately.
Yours affectionately,
William

And their wicked hearts were touched and they thought it a crying shame. So the captain of the robbers took pen and paper and wrote another letter, forging the earl's hand perfectly:

Dear Humphrey,
Take the bearer of this letter and marry her to my son immediately.
Yours affectionately,
William

He didn't know why he wrote that but he did, and popped it in the envelope, resealed it and gave it back to the girl, with a swashbuckling bow and a flourish.

The next day the girl went on to the earl's brother's house in Barnstaple, a large town mansion, where the earl's son was staying with his uncle. When the earl's brother read the letter, he gave orders for the wedding to be held at once and the girl was married to the earl's son that same day – and luckily they found each other very much to their liking.

But when, soon afterward, the earl came to visit his brother, he was dismayed to find that the very event he had tried so hard to prevent had come to pass. But even then he would not give up.

One fine day they all went riding out to Mortehoe and the earl and the girl went for a walk along the cliffs – for a fatherly chat, the earl said. As soon as they were alone, he seized her in his arms and tried to throw her over the cliff-top, but she struggled hard and begged for her life.

'I've not done you any wrong! If you will only spare my life, I'll do whatever you wish! I'll never see you or your son again!' Then the earl relented a little and he wrenched off her gold wedding ring and hurled it into the sea.

'Never let me see your face again,' he cried, 'unless you can also show me that ring!' Then he let her go and rode back to the others at Mortehoe, where he put on a great show of grief and said she had slipped and fallen from the cliff, and though they searched and searched, her body was never found.

The poor girl walked down the coast through Woolacombe, across the great sandy beach, round Baggy Point, through Croyde, then across the great dunes until she came to the estuary of the River Taw. There she walked up the riverbank until she came to a big house overlooking the river, and there she decided to stop, for she felt that the river was always, in some way, linked to her destiny. So she asked for a job and they put her in the kitchens where she worked her way up to become the cook, but because of her great sorrow she kept to herself.

One day, who should come visiting the big house but the earl, his brother and his son. She knew they were coming and her heart was in a turmoil but she thought they wouldn't see her if she stayed in the kitchen. So she set to work with a sigh, gutting and preparing a fine salmon that had been caught in the Taw only that morning. And when she cut it open, she saw something glinting in the guts and what do you think she found? Yes! It was her gold wedding ring the earl had thrown into the sea a year ago to the day. She took it out and cleaned it on her apron and put it on her finger. Then she cooked that fish as well as she knew how and it was served up to the guests. And they liked the fish so much they asked to see who had cooked it, and the servants went down to the kitchen and told the girl she was wanted up in the hall.

Up into the hall she went and when the guests saw her, they were amazed. And the earl was furious and started up to strike her – but the girl went right up to him and showed him the ring. Then at last the old earl saw that he could not fight against fate any longer and he set her in his own seat and announced to all the company that she was his son's true wife. He took his son and his daughter-in-law home to his manor house in the Taw Valley and there they all lived as happily as you would wish to yourself.

TWENTY-TWO

TOM FAGGUS THE HIGHWAYMAN

Tom Faggus is a character in R.D. Blackmore's *Lorna Doone*, but he actually lived in the seventeenth century and was a famous Exmoor highwayman who supposedly robbed from the rich and gave to the poor, like Robin Hood in days of yore. He was born at North Molton where he became a blacksmith, an honest trade he pursued for many years with some success, for he won a prize at the North Devon Show for the best shod horse. His forge, which stood next to the old Poltimore Arms, was only demolished late in the twentieth century.

In his twenties he was doing well; he owned his own property, he was a skilled craftsman and he was engaged to be married to Betsy Paramore, the beautiful daughter of a publican in South Molton. Then he fell foul of the powerful Sir Richard Bampfylde of Court Hall, who brought a lawsuit against him with the aid of his cronies in the county – magistrates, lawyers and fellow land-lords. It was said that Bampfylde held a grudge against him, that he too had an eye on the lovely Ms Paramore, that Tom was never as respectful to him as he would have wished and that he resented this young commoner, who was doing so well for himself. In any case, Bampfylde was successful and Tom Faggus was evicted from his property and unable to pursue his trade. He was now homeless and penniless, so Betsy Paramore would have nothing more to do with him and married Sir Richard.

Angry, bitter and heartbroken, Tom turned to highway robbery, a trade at which he was highly successful. He was calm and courteous, abhorred unnecessary violence, and robbed wealthy travellers without mercy while letting poor people go unharmed. In fact, he often gave money to poor widows and destitute people, which lent him his 'Robin Hood' reputation and earned him the friendship of many an Exmoor commoner.

Quite early in his new career he accosted a man on the Barnstaple road, who turned out to be his old enemy, Sir Richard Bampfylde. A lesser man would have shot the knight there and then, but Tom smiled, replaced his pistols, doffed his hat and said, 'I beg pardon, Sir Richard. I didn't see who 'twas. You may, of course, ride away unmolested. A thief does not rob a fellow thief'. And he galloped off into the darkening countryside.

Darkening it was too, for the poor. The old rights of the peasantry were eroded more and more, while the gentry were gaining more and more wealth, land and power. The rich were getting richer and the poor were getting poorer, and the only recourse for a poor man with any spirit was crime. But the forces of law and order were also getting more organised and it was only a matter of time for outlaws like Tom Faggus. The gallows was always waiting for them and 'marriage to the rope-maker's daughter' was always on the cards.

Tom had many narrow escapes and these were often effected by his famous horse, an 'enchanted' strawberry roan called Winnie. One late evening, the young highwayman was surprised by officers of the law while he was enjoying a quiet tankard of ale in the Exmoor Arms in Simonsbath. The unscrupulous landlord, greedy for the reward, had tipped them off and the officers burst in through the door and clapped the cuffs on the somewhat dozy Tom. But he gave a shrill whistle and there were sounds of splintering wood as Winnie kicked down the stable door, then smashed the inn door flat and crashed into the pub, eyes blazing, teeth snapping, hooves lashing out at the officers. It must have been terrifying in that small room and she knew who the lawmen were too. In seconds they were all slumped and moaning with bloody gashes in their heads. Tom got the key from them, unlocked the handcuffs and rode off into the night.

Another time he and Winnie were recognised in Barnstaple and, realising the hostile interest being shown to him, Tom resolved to leave town immediately and made for the sixteen-arched bridge over the River Taw leading to Sticklepath and the open country to the south. He was closely followed to the bridge by a mob of vigilantes but, once upon it, he saw that the far end was blocked by a force of constables and more volunteers. He was well and truly trapped this time!

Suddenly Winnie neighed ferociously, reared up and jumped clean over the parapet into the cold, rushing waters of the River Taw 40ft below, swimming swiftly downstream and struggling out onto the bank a mile or two downriver.

Not long afterward, intelligence reached the constable of Exford that Faggus was on his way there from Simonsbath, so he got a band of armed men together and lay in wait for the outlaw at Exford Bridge. It was a cold, wintry morning with a thick mist lying heavily across the valley and the men must have been tense and frightened as they lay crouched by the bridge. All at once a rider loomed up behind them in the mist, a gentleman in greatcoat, wig and three-cornered hat. They were still a bit nervous but the gentleman said in cultured tones, 'Hah! Are you in ambush for that double-dyed villain Tom Faggus? I'll join ye then, for the rogue robbed me once of all I had'. And he sat his horse just behind them, peering intently up the Simonsbath road. Suddenly he said, 'I say, how long have you been waitin' here in this confounded mist?'

'Oh, 'bout an hour', said the constable.

'Then you'd better discharge your guns and load them again', said the man. 'They'll have got damp in this mist and mightn't go off'.

The men duly fired their pistols into the hedge, then heard a loud double-click on the still air and, turning, saw the 'gentleman of the road' levelling his own pistols straight at them.

'Now you'd better give me those things,' he said, 'and your money, watches, tiepins and the like'.

And he robbed them all blind and galloped off in the direction of Wheddon Cross.

Tom Faggus was nearly caught again when he owned a cottage in Swimbridge, four miles east of Barnstaple, for it's a mistake for a highwayman to be a householder and one of Tom's neighbours grew suspicious of his comings and goings, usually at dusk. The neighbour scrutinised the 'Wanted' posters in Barnstaple and informed the authorities, for the reward money was now 500 guineas – enough to set a man up in a tidy business.

Tom's house was surrounded by officers and volunteers and a siege began. It ended when his hat appeared from the chimney and everyone fired at it. It dropped and a cry of 'Faggus is dead!' went up – but as the mob burst in through the front door, Tom burst out through the back, already mounted on Winnie the 'enchanted steed' and made off while the posse were reloading.

Tom was at last tracked down to an alehouse in Exbridge, three miles from Dulverton. A constable dressed in drag as an old beggar woman shuffled into the room where Faggus was sitting. Tom, with his customary kindness, ordered a mug of ale for the old biddy but the constable knocked the chair from under him, others rushed in, fastened a rope to his ankles and hoisted him up to the bacon-rack, where Tom gave his shrill whistle. But it was in vain. At the moment Tom was secured, Winnie was shot dead in the stable.

Tom was taken to Taunton Gaol and tried the next day at the Assizes. He was found guilty of highway robbery and hanged a week later in Taunton marketplace.

'Yeoland', his house at Swimbridge, still stands and is reputed to contain a horseshoe once belonging to Winnie, his celebrated 'enchanted' strawberry roan. A gun of his is preserved at St Anne's Chapel Museum in Barnstaple, as a memorial to a highwayman who never committed one act of cruelty, who assuaged many a poor person's poverty, who was kind-hearted and daring and who was driven to a life of crime by the manifold injustices of the rich.

TWENTY-THREE

WITCH HARES

'RUN, GRANNY, RUN!'

The most common tradition concerning witches in the West Country was their ability to transform themselves into hares. In 1885, at Rose Ash near South Molton, a man shot a hare with pellets made from a silver sixpence and the same day a suspected witch of the district had suspicious wounds in her leg, according to Vol. 57 of the *Transactions of the Devonshire Association*.

Mrs Bray, writing in 1833 in her book *The Borders of the Tamar and the Tavy*, tells of a witch of Tavistock who, whenever she was short of money, turned herself into a hare and then sent her little grandson to tell the local hunt that he'd seen a hare at a particular spot. For this information the grandson always got a sixpence. After this trick had been played many times and the hare never caught, the hunt smelt a witch and they called in a clergyman and a magistrate, and all agreed to get the hunt in readiness as soon as granny and grandson left their cottage, of which they were to be informed by an unfriendly neighbour.

The hare was spotted, the hunt was in hot pursuit at once and the hare was hard pressed. The boy, forgetting himself, cried out, 'Run, granny, run! Run for your life!' For a moment the hare lost the pursuit and dashed straight to the cottage, where it got in through a little hole at the bottom of the door – presumably the hare-flap – but the huntsmen were not far behind and they galloped up to the old woman's cottage, dismounted and tried to break the door down. But they could not, despite the combined efforts of a score of burly squires. Then the magistrate and the vicar arrived and the combined might of law and Church proved too much for the spells that bound the door and they all burst in and tumbled up the stairs.

Granny was on the bed, bleeding, covered with wounds, panting for breath. 'I bain't a hare!' she cried. 'Damn you all for interfering,

snot-nosed bastards! Leave I alone, you upper-class sods!' and such-like, railing at the whole party with unconcealed venom.

'Call up the hounds!' shouted the master of the hunt. 'Let us see what they take her to be! Hah! We may have another hunt yet!' At this the old woman broke down and begged for quarter and her little grandson fell to his knees and pleaded for mercy, saying they were only poor folk trying to make a penny or two.

The huntsmen would have dragged the old hag before the mag-istrates straight away but the parson himself pleaded for her, say-ing there would be no one to look after the little boy if she were imprisoned. The hunt relented, provided she were granted mercy along with a good whipping, which being agreed, the master pro-ceeded to administer.

The old woman escaped a far worse fate at that time but a year later she was put on trial for bewitching a young woman and mak-ing her spit pins and, this business of turning into a hare being brought up and held as further evidence of her witchcraft, she was burned at the stake. What happened to the poor little grandson we do not know, but I doubt if he harboured any more respect for those in power.

MOLL STANCOMBE

On the other side of the moor comes a tale from Chagford, told by an old woman living near the town to the author of a very rare book, *Dartmoor and its Borders* (1873).

Moll Stancombe lived in a hut close to the moor and could change from an old woman to a hare at will. When she was 'Puss' she was very big, whitish grey and no one could catch or kill her. A doctor of Moretonhampstead had a wonderful pack of hounds and coursed her one day, but the hare ran away with such speed, the dogs might just as well have been standing still. The fame of this hare spread and a certain squire made a bet that his harriers would kill her. They found her sitting on some furze stubble and away she ran, the hounds after her. She was chased for nearly an hour and the hounds all but caught up with her, when she dived into a tangled break of furze and gorse, startling a young hare out of it, which the dogs killed and then refused to try further, as they had done their job and killed the game.

A rival witch, envious of Moll's fame, advised shooting her with a silver bullet so a man called Giles moulded some silver into a bullet and went out in the moonlight to have a shot at Puss, whom he found eating clover. He fired at her but the gun burst and blew his hand off. Giles was a cast-off lover of Moll's, and she was heard to say afterward, 'Sarve 'en right!'

Then a Widecombe witch was consulted and she said that the hare should be coursed with a spayed bitch. One fine, moonlit evening when Puss was again enjoying her clover, such an animal was set upon her and the chase was on, but it was curious; for while the hare seemed unable to get away from the dog, the dog could not come up with the hare. Finally, Puss tried to scramble through a thick hedge and the dog leaped at her and tore off a piece of flesh from her rump. The dog's owner went straight to Moll Stancombe's hut, but the door was barred so he peered in through the window and there was Moll, attaching a large piece of plaster to a wound on her rump. This confirmed the general belief that the hare was Moll but she seemed to have learned her lesson, for the hare was never seen again.

DEWER HUNTS A HARE

Back over the other side of the moor, there was once an old woman who woke up in the middle of the night, convinced it was almost morning and time to set off for Tavistock market. She duly set out over the moor on her horse, laden with panniers full of produce to sell. There was a bright full moon, which had probably woken her up, so she saw quite clearly a hare racing toward her across the tussocks and the stones. To her surprise it made straight for her and jumped up into her lap, and at the same time she heard a baying of hounds and a galloping of hooves from the same direction.

She just had time to thrust the hare into one of her panniers when, to her horror, up rode a black hooded rider on a black horse, surrounded by huge black hounds with glaring red eyes, barely kept under control by the rider's whip, which seemed to be made of blackened tongues sewn together. Hardly daring to look, the old woman yet sensed there was no face inside the hood and she saw a cloven hoof in one of the stirrups.

'Excuse me, ma'am,' said Dewer with perfect civility, 'but did you notice the hare we are hunting and did you see which way it went?'

'Yes sir, I did', she replied with trembling voice. 'It went that way, back up over Standon toward Hare Tor', she said, half turning in her saddle and pointing back over her left shoulder.

'Thank you kindly, ma'am', said Dewer with a bow and he lashed his dogs with the whip of tongues and galloped off in that direction. As soon as they were over the brow of Cudlipp Down, the hare leaped out of the pannier and changed into a beautiful young woman, who held the reins of the old woman's horse and said:

> I cannot thank you enough. You have saved me from eternal torment. I am not of your race but for doing a dreadful wrong among my own people I was condemned to be hunted by Dewer and his dogs for ever unless I could get behind them. Now, thanks to you, I have managed it and I can go back to my own world. You shall be rewarded for your kindness. Your hens will lay two eggs instead of one, your cows will give twofold the milk all the year round and I shall give you a tongue that can never be bested in any dispute, neither with your husband, nor with any other man.

With that the young woman faded away into the lightening air and the old woman went on her way to Tavistock market. There, she did better than she had ever done before, and when she got home there were two eggs instead of one in every nest, the cows gave twice the milk they used to and that evening at supper, when she mentioned a new silk petticoat she wanted for her Sunday best, the garment was at once promised as a gift. From that time on she prospered and no man was a match for her tongue, not even the gypsies at Goosey Fair!

Twenty-four

The White Bird of the Oxenhams

Not far from the shaded banks of the River Taw, between South Tawton and North Tawton, lies the old manor farmhouse of the Oxenhams, an ancient Devonian family to whom a strange tradition is attached. It is said that a white bird or a bird with a white breast hovers over their beds when they are about to die. The earliest account of this is in a tract of 1641, *A True Relation of an Apparition etc.*, published by James Oxenham. This states that in 1635 his son John, who was twenty-two and 6½ft tall, fell sick and died, 'to whom two dayes before hee yeelded up his soule to God, there appeared the likenesse of a bird with a white breast, hovering over him'. This was witnessed by two reliable household servants, their names on the document being Elisabeth Frost and Joan Tooker or Tucker, who reported the appearances first to the vicar and then to the bishop.

Two days later Thomazine, the wife of John's brother James, died having also been visited by the white bird. Two days after that, Thomazine's sister Rebeccah, aged eight, died after seeing the bird hover over her and this was followed on the same day by the death of James and Thomazine's baby, once the white bird had fluttered over her cradle. Four of the family had died and those with them had all seen the bird, while four other members of the family had fallen ill at the same time and had recovered, the white bird coming nowhere near them. It was then remembered that 'the said bird appeared to Grace, the Grandmother of the said John, over her death-bed – in the yeare of our Redemption, 1618'.

The Stuart historian Thomas Westcote, who lived in the parish of Zeal Monachorum where the Oxenham house is situated, close to South Zeal, makes no mention of the apparition in his book *A View of Devonshire* (1630). However, James Howell, in *Familiar Letters* (1645), wrote that he saw a memorial tablet to four Oxenhams that mentioned the bird in 1632, but that date is three years earlier than the above version of the story and the names are different. This marble tablet has never been seen since, so there is a mystery there. Prince mentions the visitation in his *Worthies of Devon* (1701), and there have been other reports of it down through the years.

In 1743 William Oxenham, who was then sixty-four, saw the white bird fluttering outside his bedroom window and declared defiantly that he would 'cheat the bird'. But he didn't – he died.

At Sidmouth in the early 1800s, an Oxenham died in a room where people who knew nothing of the legend saw a white bird fly across the room and disappear into a drawer.

In 1873 a G.N. Oxenham was spending Christmas at a house in Kensington, preparing for his death, when he saw a white bird perched on a tree outside his window. His nephew, the Revd Henry Oxenham, said that his aunt and the nurse had heard flutterings inside the chamber, while the dying man's daughter and a friend of hers, who knew nothing of the legend, heard a commotion outside. They opened the window and there was a strange white bird, larger than a pigeon, perched on a bush and some tipsy workmen were trying to drive it away by throwing their hats at it. A week later G.N. Oxenham died and his wife and daughter heard the fluttering again quite clearly.

In 1892 another member of the family told the Devon writer Sarah Hewett, author of *Nummits and Crummits*, that the bird had appeared to him and that his father had died, so perhaps the bird itself was getting elderly and confused.

In 1896 a pseudo-Gothic ballad purporting to describe the
origin and first appearance of the white bird was found in the
housekeeper's commonplace book at Oxenham Manor, and this
was copied by Miss E. Gibbs of South Tawton and sent to the
Devonshire Association, who published it in their *Transactions* for
that year. It is a typical load of late Victorian tosh, beginning:

> Where lofty hills in grandeur meet
> And Taw meandering flows,
> There is a calm and sweet retreat
> Where once a mansion rose.

It tells the story of Margaret, only daughter and sole heiress of
Sir James Oxenham. She was courted by a local landowner called
Bertram who, in an accident, was hit on the head and became an
imbecile. Margaret was at first inconsolable but, 'consoling time
healed the heart with anguish grieved', especially as she was then
wooed by Sir John of Roxamcave, who was 'handsome, young and
brave' and they appointed their marriage day.

The night before, while Sir James was talking to his future son-in-law at the stag party held at Oxenham Manor:

> He saw a silvery breasted bird
> Fly o'er the festive throng.

Next day in church they were all ranged round the altar and the marriage service had begun:

> When Margaret, with terrific screams,
> Made all with horror start.
> Oh heavens! her blood in torrents streams –
> A dagger's in her heart.
>
> Behind stood Bertram, who then drew
> Away the reeking blade
> And frantically laughed to view
> The life-blood of the maid.

Then, crying:

> Now marry me, proud maid!
> Thy blood with mine shall wed.

...Bertram stabbed himself and fell upon the bride. They both died, while the phantom white bird hovered over them, waiting to bear Margaret's last breath to the skies. Deathless verse, unfortunately.

In more recent times, Theo Brown talked to an old lady of the Oxenham family in 1969, who was extremely sceptical and did not believe in the tradition. Most emphatically she did not believe that her uncle saw the bird at a farm on the edge of Exmoor when her father lay dying, for this uncle of hers had always been highly strung and imaginative. The apparition is known as a 'fetch', presumably because it 'fetches' you away.

Twenty-five

Buried Treasure

Cadbury and Dolbury

There are many folk tales of buried treasure all over the country and that is usually just what they are – folk tales – but once in a blue moon there is substance at the heart of them. However, no one has yet found the hoards implied by the following old rhyme:

> If Cadbury Castle and Dolbury Hill dolven were,
> All England would plough with a golden share.

Both are hill forts and in the 1950s an old lady at Cullompton confided to Ralph Whitlock, the writer and farmer, that they both contained buried treasure. A fiery dragon was supposed to fly every night between the two of them, guarding the treasure. Cadbury, of course, is a name given to several possible sites of King Arthur's Camelot in the West Country, and all of them are said to be hollow, to hold buried treasure and to be guarded by sleeping, Dark Age warriors.

FARDEL HALL

Fardel Hall lies just to the north-west of Ivybridge, on the southern edge of Dartmoor, and legend has it that the manor once belonged to Sir Walter Raleigh. Legend also maintains that he hid a vast quantity of treasure in the grounds of Fardel Hall before he made his last journey to London, as he had a premonition of what might befall him there. Legend also says that in one of the fields of Fardel Hall, there once stood a long stone – like a standing stone – on one side of which were inscribed the words:

> Between this stone and Fardel Hall
> There lies more gold than the devil could haul.

The field was not unprotected, however. It could not be cultivated or dug. If you tried to stick a spade or a pick into it, the tool would break, the earth would shake and a loud rumbling and moaning would be heard. But during the seventeenth century, the Fardel Stone was taken into the courtyard of the hall, where it was used as a hitching-post for horses and later, in the eighteenth century, the owner of the hall had it sent to the British Museum in London and there it stands to this day, so the clue written on its side is no longer of much use.

You might try scouting round the fields of Fardel Hall with a pendulum, I suppose, but there is one more guardian of the treasure, for the field is patrolled by a silkie, a household spirit in the form of a beautiful young woman with long, golden hair, wearing a long, silken gown. This spirit, which is not human, is rarely seen and it's bad luck even to set eyes on such a creature. Mostly people have only heard the rustling of its silk dress, but if you were to attempt to get the treasure or even if you were skulking round the field with that intention, Silkie would glide up behind you – her silk rustling softly in the night – and strangle you, slowly and gently but inexorably.

TROW HILL

A similar spirit haunted a field at the top of Trow Hill, just by the main road from Exeter to Lyme Regis, not far beyond Sidford. This was a lady in grey who was sometimes seen gliding over the surface of the field, apparently searching for something. In 1811 the yeoman farmer who owned the land was ploughing this field when one of his oxen sank into the ground. He managed to get the beast out, with a great deal of trouble, and then found to his amazement that the cavity thus revealed contained a large amount of treasure. The farmer, who was a poor man, kept this find to himself, telling anyone who asked about the sudden hollow in the field that it was an old smuggler's hiding place and that it was full of nothing but earth and stones.

Some weeks later, a collection of large boxes was carted down to Sidford and then transported by coach to London. The farmer became noticeably better off and when his children grew up and got married, each one of them received £1,500 as a wedding gift. After the discovery of this hoard, the lady in grey ceased to haunt the field, her task of guarding the treasure being over. This story is set down in *A Descriptive Sketch of Sidmouth* by T.H. Mogridge, published in 1836.

DOWNHOUSE

Mrs Bray's *The Borders of the Tamar and the Tavy* (1833), contains the story of Downhouse, a large farm standing half a mile west of Tavistock. The house was rebuilt in 1822 but the original building was very ancient and was haunted by a very tall man. The family who lived there were well aware of the ghost and the hour of the night when it appeared, and took good care to be in bed before then.

One night, however, one of the children was very ill and asked his mother, who was watching by his bedside, for some water. The woman poured out a glassful from the jug standing on the bedside table but the boy did not want that and insisted on fresh water from the pump in the yard. This put the poor woman in a quandary, for it was the time of night when the ghost walked. The sick child again pleaded for fresh water from the pump so the mother, swallowing her fear for the sake of her darling son, said, 'In the name of God I will go down', and went quickly from the room.

As she descended the stairs, she thought she saw out of the corner of her eye a tall shadow following her down and as she walked swiftly across the yard, she clearly heard footsteps behind her – just as she reached the pump, she felt a hand on her shoulder. Terrified, she turned and there was the shadowy figure of a tall man standing right in front of her.

Plucking up all her courage, she said, 'In the name of God, why troublest thou me?' The ghost replied:

> It is well for thee that thou hast spoken to me in the name of God
> or else I should have injured thee. Now do as I tell thee and be not
> afraid, for this is the last time I shall trouble this world. Come with
> me and I shall direct thee to a something which shall remove this
> pump, for under it is a concealed treasure.

Well, whatever the 'something' was, it removed the pump without
too much difficulty and in the cavity thus revealed, there was a
great heap of gold and silver coins. The ghost then said:

> This treasure is to be used to improve the farm and anyone foolish
> enough to try and take the money away from you will come to grief.
> You should now take the fresh water to your sick child, who will
> soon recover from his illness on account of his mother's courage and
> trust in God

Mind you, how she filled the jug with the pump removed, good-
ness only knows! But suddenly a cock crowed loudly in the farmyard and the apparition, on that time-honoured signal, began to
grow less and less distinct, rose slowly up into the air, became a
small, bright cloud and gradually disappeared, drifting off into the
lightening air of dawn. It was never seen again and the old farm of
Downhouse prospered ever afterward.

RADFORD

In the story of John Fitz we heard how after his death his wife, Mary,
married Sir Christopher Harris of Radford. The Harrises were a powerful and wealthy family in the parish of Plymstock and Sir Christopher was a Member of Parliament for Plymouth and a personal friend
of Sir Francis Drake. At Radford he stored lots of gold and silver bars
that Drake had brought back as plunder from the Spanish Main.

In 1618, as Vice-Admiral of Devon, he held Sir Walter Raleigh
prisoner at Radford upon the latter's return from his ill-fated voy-

age to Guiana. He must have done so with reluctance, for Raleigh was well-loved throughout Devon. Sir Christopher died in 1625, when Radford passed to his great-nephew, John Harris.

John was on the Royalist side in the Civil War and while Plymouth was besieged by Sir Richard Grenville, the King's General in the South West, he bore the rank of major-general of infantry and kept a garrison at the house. In 1645 the siege was broken, Grenville was defeated and had to flee for his life and Radford was occupied by the Roundheads, who were eager to get their hands on the Harris silver plate, but it had disappeared. The house was stripped and virtually taken apart, oak panelling torn from the walls, floorboards taken up and even the plaster hacked away but the silver plate was not found.

The fate of the plate remained a mystery until 6 December 1827, when some farm workers were enlarging a potato cave on a farm at Brixton, two miles from Radford. There and then the dream of all treasure-seekers came true – they unearthed the long-lost treasure: twenty-three pieces of silver plate, dating from between 1581 to 1602. In 1886 it was sold at auction for £1,225 16s, then bought again straight afterward for £1,900. Radford House was demolished in 1937 and the property was turned over to building developers, who built a modern housing estate on it.

Twenty-six

Ghost Houses

CHAGFORD

In Devon there are houses which are only seen occasionally – phantom houses. In *Haunted Britain* by Elliott O'Donnell, there is the story of a cottage within walking distance of Chagford, which looked so charming in the summer sunshine with its roses round the door and neat lawns, that two Edwardian ladies from London who chanced across it whilst visiting the area decided it was their dream cottage and that they must try to rent rooms in it or even lease the whole cottage. They knocked at the door, which was opened by a pretty little girl dressed all in white, who invited them into a well-furnished, immaculately clean sitting room and went to fetch her mother. While waiting, they looked around the room and saw a huge white cat lying on the hearth rug, gazing steadily at them with big green eyes. Uneasily, they turned to look at the window, where hung a cage in which perched a strange looking blackbird, which stared at them malevolently.

The little girl came back in with her mother, an unusually tall woman elegantly dressed in white, wearing expensive but somewhat bizarre jewellery. She did not seem the kind of person you would find in a country cottage. Her eyes were a vivid blue, like the child's and, like the cat and the bird, mother and daughter kept their eyes fixed upon the visitors.

'We were wondering,' said one of the ladies hesitantly, aware that something odd was going on, 'whether you might have two rooms that we could rent for a holiday?'

'I regret to say,' said the lady of the house, 'that all my rooms are at present occupied, but I should be able to accommodate you later in the year, perhaps in September, if you should still wish for a holiday on Dartmoor then'. Her voice was cultivated and welcoming.

'We should like it very much', said the other lady and they made a provisional arrangement for two weeks in September.

When they left the cottage and had gone a little way back toward Chagford, they realised that they had no idea of the lady's name, nor even the name of the cottage; but it seemed silly to go back and admit this so they made careful note of the way as they retraced their steps to Chagford and were sure they could find the place again.

In September they returned to the quaint little Dartmoor town as arranged and made their way straight to the dream cottage. Dream it had been! A heap of stones and rubble covered with nettles was all that the site had to show and it was clear that it had been like that for fifty years or more. When they returned bewilderedly to Chagford, some locals they got talking to in the Three Crowns told them that there were cottages in those parts that only manifested themselves once every ten or twelve years, which was handy when it came to paying the rates!

BUCKFASTLEIGH

Three young girls visiting Devon as tourists with their parents once got lost near Buckfastleigh and came upon an isolated cottage by the roadside. It was twilight and there was a light burning inside. They looked in through the window and saw an old man and an old woman sitting on a bench by the fire. Then the cottage vanished and they found themselves standing at the roadside in complete darkness, staring into the hedge. They finally found their way home and walked out from Buckfastleigh the next day; all that could be seen on the spot were a few stones and hummocks marking the foundations. This phenomenon was well-known locally. People who lived in the area called it the 'phantom cottage of the moor', and when it was real, back in the nineteenth century, it had a nasty reputation for evil goings-on.

MARY MORTON'S STORY

Mary Morton of Chagford, a dear friend and formidable director of amateur dramatics, told me a curious story on Halloween in 2000. It was a first-hand experience. A few years before, she was driving over the foothills of the moor near Ashburton, down a wiggly little lane that joins the Dartmeet road, when she looked through a gate on her left into a field that was normally just full of ragwort and brambles. To her surprise, and she stopped the car because of it, the undergrowth had all been cleared away and at the far end of the field stood an imposing Elizabethan manor house, where there had never been a house before. She even wondered if it was a film set. Then she thought, perhaps trees and undergrowth now cut down had hidden it from view; so she drove on and thought no more about it. But the next time she drove down that lane, she looked into the field and the house was not there. Later she heard that a new housing estate was being built in the field and that it was going to be called 'Manor Field Gardens'.

HARLESTON

In 1939 two sisters saw the 'phantom manor of Harleston' near Stoke Fleming. They lived at Start House, about a mile from

Slapton. A small lane went on to Kingsbridge, about five miles away. This lane led over a stream and so on up the valley on high ground, with the country on the other side of the valley sloping up through the trees. It was about a mile up the lane from Start House that the two ladies saw the phantom house. It was a November afternoon, rather misty and damp. They stopped to lean over a farm gate and admire the view. Suddenly, one sister said to the other, 'I thought there was no house here!' They looked across the valley and there in the trees was a great manor house with big arched doors. As they watched in amazement, more buildings appeared among the trees at the side of the house. They knew it wasn't real. They knew this countryside well, having walked this way dozens of times, and they knew there was no house there. Anyway, it didn't look real. It had no substance. As they talked and watched for about five minutes, the house gradually faded away.

Several people living in Start House before them had heard horses galloping down the lane but although they had gone out to look, no one had ever actually seen them, only heard them go past. No doubt they were ghost horses from the ghost house! The strange thing is, there has never been a large manor house or any kind of dwelling at all at this particular place.

DOLTON

And finally: 'the Ghost-House at Dolton, or Mr Ackroyd's Adventure' – with apologies to all concerned. (For I got this story from Katherine Briggs, who got it from Augustus Hare, who got it from Mrs Pole-Carew, who heard it from Dr E.W. Benson, then Bishop of Truro, who was told it by Mr Ackroyd himself.)

Dr E.W. Benson was sitting at a table in a country house at a weekend party. Two young men were sitting with him, one of them being Mr Ackroyd. He was talking of a place he knew in the County of Devon, close to the village of Dolton, and how a particular adventure always befell him at a certain gate there.

'Yes,' said the other young man, 'your horse shies at that spot, then turns down a lane next to it.'

'Why yes,' said Mr Ackroyd, 'but how do you know?'

'Well, the same thing always happens to me at that place.'

'And then I come to a gateway', continued Mr Ackroyd.

'Exactly so.'

'And on one occasion, rode through it and came to a house.'

'Ah! Well, there I do not follow you', said the young gentleman, looking puzzled.

'It was a good few years ago', went on Mr Ackroyd. 'I was a boy, out riding with my father. It was Christmastime and we were staying with friends at Dolton. There had been a heavy snowfall the previous night but the day was bright and cold. We went out for a ride in the afternoon and were just making our way back to the village when we came to the gate I have mentioned, an ordinary wooden gate leading into thick, tangled woodland. All at once our horses shied at the gate and turned off down this dark lane and, being in the mood for an adventure, we gave them their heads.'

'It was then quite late in the afternoon, beginning to get dark and, what with the darkness of the lane itself, surrounded as it was by this dense woodland, we could scarcely see where we were going, except for the whiteness of the snow-covered lane against the darkness of the woods and a thin fingernail of a moon that showed herself from time to time through a ragged cover of cloud. All of a sudden we reached another gate, closed across the lane and beyond it was a curving, gravelled drive and set back within the trees a great house, brilliantly lit up.'

'When we had opened the gate and were leading our horses up the drive, we saw that there was evidently some sort of banquet or house-party going on inside, for through the large windows, shining with the light of a thousand candles, were throngs of figures moving to and fro, but all were in medieval dress so naturally we thought it was a masquerade.'

'We walked up to the house to inquire our way and after speaking to a footman, who spoke to some sort of major-domo, who no doubt spoke to someone else, the owner of the house himself came out to speak to us. He too was in medieval dress, all red and black velvet robes and very handsome he was too, in a rather dark, saturnine sort of way. He entreated us, as chance had brought us his way that night, to stay a while, to come in and partake of his hospitality; but my father pleaded that we were obliged to go on, that people were expecting us, that they might well be getting worried already, that it was impossible to stay. I admit I was relieved, for although he was excessively civil to us, there was something I did not like about the owner of this house. His face was cruel and mocking, almost sardonic, and there was an aura about him I detested. Even the horses were nervous in his presence.'

'Finally, he said that if we really must go we should at least allow him to send a footman with us, to take us back to the right road. When we got back to the top of the lane my father gave the footman half a crown, but it was only when we had gone some distance toward Dolton and could see the lights of the village before us that I was able to say, in a rather small voice, "Father, did you see what happened to that half crown?"'

'"Yes my boy, I did", replied my father and said no more. You see, the half crown had fallen right through the footman's hand and had lain there, glinting on the snow, and the footman himself had seemed rather to fade into the gathering dark than simply turn back down the lane.'

'The following week, my father made many enquiries, both in Dolton and in the County Archive office in Exeter. Oh, the lane really exists, as you know but, as you also know, there is no house there now, nor any sign of one. But there was a house there once, in the fourteenth century, an evil house inhabited by some very wicked people; a brother and sister who were guilty of the most horrible blasphemies and unnatural practices, who danced naked upon the altar in the chapel and who held the most vile orgies in the house. It was said that any traveller chancing upon that place by night, who had the ill luck to be lured inside, was never seen again. Well, fortunately we weren't and that, I'm glad to say, was the extent of my adventure.'

Thus said Mr Ackroyd – and dinner was ready.

Twenty-seven

Haunted Roads

Sidford

In Devon, as well as 'ghost houses' that do not exist, there are stretches of road that appear to be haunted. Several are 'shy-points' for horses, as in the account of the Dolton ghost house – particular places in the road to which horses are unusually sensitive. One shy-point is on the bridge over the River Sid at Sidford. Although it is a modern bridge, the old pack-horse bridge by the side of it is now used by pedestrians and equestrians. Theo Brown, the folklore recorder for the Devonshire Association, once lived beside it in the Old Tannery, and a friend of hers used to ride past regularly on her big black horse to go to the village blacksmith. The horse always shied at the bridge and Miss Brown's friend thought it was because during the Civil War, five cavaliers had been killed there in a skirmish and were buried by the bridge. The horse could sense their spirits.

Beetor Cross

Another shy-point is at Beetor Cross, on the Moretonhampstead to Princetown road. There is an old granite cross up in the hedge there and a local tradition maintains that a spectral hand reaches out from nowhere to grab the bridles of passing horses, causing them to shy and unseat their riders.

Beetor Cross is also known as 'Watching Place', and there are a number of possible reasons for this: firstly, it was the site of a gallows in medieval times and this was where the relatives of the hanged man would watch and wait for permission to remove the corpse; secondly, it was where the highwayman John Fall would watch and wait to leap out at travellers; thirdly, close to the cross lay a flat slab of granite upon which people would leave food for plague victims at nearby Puddaven farm; fourthly, during the Napoleonic Wars a watch was kept here for French and American prisoners breaking their parole from Moretonhampstead; and finally, this was the place where local British warriors watched for the invading Saxon army. So the spectral hand could belong to a hanged man, a highwayman, a plague victim, a prisoner of war or a Dark Age warrior – take your pick.

LONG LANE

'Long Lane' from Hay Tor crosses the trans-Dartmoor road at Beetor Cross and continues down to Chagford, and along here is another strange spot. The narrow, high-banked lane leads down under the trees to a little stone bridge, then winds up a hill on the other side. Car drivers, cyclists and motorcyclists have experienced uncomfortable sensations here: fear, panic, terror and nausea, sometimes accompanied by an obnoxious smell. The feelings get stronger the deeper into the dip you go, and recede as you climb up out of it. No one knows the reason for this unpleasant manifestation, though I did hear that a walker once saw a man leading a horse and cart over the hump-backed bridge, then watched the whole lot fade into the hedge. But it is very close to Beetor Cross so maybe there's some spillage.

DE BATHE CROSS

However, the previous story reminds me of de Bathe Cross and the roads leading to it, something to which I have already alluded. I have two eye-witness accounts here, though one of them saw nothing. A friend of ours who used to live in North Tawton and with whom I used to morris dance, was a long-distance lorry driver and a biker, and was not prone to be afraid of anything; but he was driving home one night in his car down the steep hill past de Bathe Moor toward the dip by the station and Speke's Farm, when he began to experience just such sensations as I have described – an awful smell, nausea and terror. These mounted rapidly the closer to the bottom of the dip he came, until he was almost overcome by them and thought he might even pass out; but as he drove on through the dip and up the other side toward de Bathe Cross, the sensation receded and by the time he reached the crossroads he was more or less back to normal, apart from being severely shaken. When he got home – and his wife has corroborated this – he almost fell in through the door, collapsed onto a chair and asked for a good, strong cup of sweet tea. His wife had never seen him in such a state and he's the sort of chap you'd want at your side if you were surrounded by half a dozen muggers. In fact, you'd pity the muggers.

The other person who had a nasty experience while approaching de Bathe Cross was the lady from Bow who delivered our vegetables (we called her the Veg Lady). This time she was driving along the main road from Bow to de Bathe Cross when, as she approached the crossroads, she too had those same sensations: a really horrible smell, a feeling that she was about to be violently sick and a rising fear, akin to panic. At some point, she looked in her rear-view mirror and saw, or thought she saw, the face of a devil leering at her from the back of the van. What reminded her of this incident was coming in through our front door and seeing the mask of a devil that my wife, Wendy, had just made for a mummer's play staring at her from the bookcase by the door.

She gave a big start, said, 'Oh my God!' and told us of her experience there and then, which had occurred some time before, but she had erased it from her mind, simply telling herself she had been 'seeing things', as you do. Once she'd got to the crossroads and turned right to North Tawton, all was back to normal.

THE A38

The A38 seems to be particularly affected. Theo Brown says that there is a strange man in a grey mackintosh who appears on that road west of Wellington, pointing a torch downward. Sometimes he thumbs a lift, sometimes he just stands there before vanishing. I wonder what happens if you stop to pick him up.

On the A38 going over Haldon Hill to the south of Exeter, there is a phantom hitch-hiker, an old tramp who vanishes when you stop to give him a lift. As the same road approaches Chudleigh, there is a sharp dip in the road where anyone riding down it on a bicycle would find themselves accompanied by a tall, running figure holding its arms out level with its shoulders and flapping them, scaring the riders so that they swerve and crash into the hedge. Theo said there had been several such occurrences but none lately, and wondered if the 'flapper' had transferred his attentions to the new road, i.e. the dual carriageway that now bypasses the town.

On the A38 near Plymouth there are phantom hands that wave across your windscreen at night in the rain, mirroring the windscreen wipers. Perhaps these are the 'hairy hands', updated and trying to catch up with the twenty-first century!

MILTON COMBE

In a letter to the *Western Morning News* of 2 January 1971, someone (unnamed) was driving down to the Who'd Have Thought

It Inn in Milton Combe, down the steep, narrow hill shaded by trees with a sharp right-hand bend at the bottom, when they saw a horse and cart coming round the corner. As they reversed up the road to make room, they saw the horse and cart emerge into the sunlight and gradually fade away. When they told the landlady at the inn, she said, 'Oh, that's the last of the old carters. By the fire there's the chair he used to sit in and that's his whip hanging on the wall'.

THE A386: MERTON TO MEETH

And finally, a strange tale was told to me by my friend the architect. He said it happened to a friend of his – well, it always does, doesn't it? This involved the stretch of road between Merton and Meeth on the A386 from Great Torrington to Okehampton. As you leave Merton, heading south, you go round a left-hand bend and start driving up a long straight stretch with the Clinton estate on your left. My friend's friend was running pottery classes in Torrington and had to drive home to Hatherleigh late at night.

The first time he entered the long straight he suddenly became convinced that there was someone sitting behind him on the back seat. The feeling was so strong he dared not look behind, nor in the rear-view mirror, but simply put his foot down and drove as fast as he could. As he drove out of the straight and on into Meeth, the feeling left him and the presence departed from the car, but he was still left feeling nervous.

The second time he began to drive on that section of road, he all at once found himself out of his body, flying through the air about 20-30ft above the car, following it along and looking down on it, seeing himself driving and analysing how well he was driving – 'I took that stretch a bit fast'. The moment he came out of the straight and started driving round the bends toward Meeth, he was back in his body in the car and now well and truly frightened.

The third time, he was already apprehensive as he drove out of Merton, and as he entered the straight the feeling that someone or something was in the car with him was overpowering. There was also a really obnoxious smell, a truly horrible odour that made him feel sick to the pit of his stomach, and a sensation of malevolent evil in the car. It was too much for him. He stopped the car in the middle of the straight, got out and ran down the road away from it. Then he flagged down another car going his way, for he was still horribly conscious of being on the haunted stretch of road, and got a lift back to Hatherleigh. The next day, his wife drove him out to the abandoned car and he was able to drive it home. The manifestations did not occur during the day.

The next time he had to go to Torrington, his wife went with him and on the way home she drove. He sat next to her in the passenger seat. They drove through Merton, went past the saw-mills on the left, round a couple of bends and came into the straight stretch. His wife glanced at him. He appeared to be all right, though he was sitting very tensely and his face was white. She drove through the straight and into the bends toward Meeth, turned to him and said, 'There, that was all right, wasn't it?' He looked at her with an absolutely ghastly face and said, 'No, it wasn't. It was all there, same as last time. I thought I was going to die. In fact, I nearly passed out'. He cancelled his pottery classes and never drove on that stretch of road again.

My friend the architect says that stretch of road does have a reputation with other drivers, and that even he is uneasy about driving along it. Another friend of mine says we ought to try it late at night. I'm not so sure.

TWENTY EIGHT

CRUEL COPINGER

It was a dark and stormy night at Marsland Mouth. A tempest was blowing up from the south-west, with mountainous waves thundering on the shore. In the flashes of lightning the watchers on the beach could see, through the hanging veils of rain, a strange vessel with broken masts and tattered sails being blown onto the rocks. Many of the watchers were waiting for the worldly goods the wreck would bring them but among them were good folk, Christian souls concerned for the saving of survivors, including an old woman in a red cloak and a young woman on a grey horse, Dinah Hamlyn of Galsham.

As the doomed ship rolled in toward the rocks, they all saw a Herculean figure standing at the wheel, who suddenly stripped off his coat, boots and breeches and dived over the side into the raging turmoil of the sea. For several minutes they thought he was lost but then he rose again, battling against the sea, riding the waves like a Triton until, with a bound, he stood upright on the sand – a Viking, tall, fierce and half-naked, his long, fair hair and beard dripping with salt water. He pushed his way through the astonished crowd, snatched the red cloak from the old woman, wrapped it round his glistening torso and leaped up onto the crupper of Dinah Hamlyn's horse, throwing his brawny arms round the startled girl, seizing the reins and shouting some foreign words at the horse, which galloped off into the night. Some people say the ship disappeared as soon as the man did.

Strange was Dinah's homecoming that night, galloping up to her father's door in the embrace of a tall, half-naked stranger, but the man was made welcome, as any shipwrecked soul on that coast would be and was kitted out in an old suit of Mr Hamlyn's – a velveteen coat and moleskin breeches. Dressed, he seemed quite civilised and Dinah was quite taken by him, flattered that he should have chosen her. He said his name was John Copinger, a Dane from a wealthy family, that he had gone to sea to escape a marriage to a titled lady not to his liking. This romantic circumstance endeared him even further to Dinah and he soon settled himself into family life at Galsham. His manners were impeccable, his conversation wide-ranging and he wrote many letters to people of rank in Denmark, receiving in reply money and means for his return to that country.

All at once Mr Hamlyn became ill. No one knew the cause, not even the old country doctor they got in for him and he declined rapidly. On his deathbed he implored the handsome and capable Dane to look after his wife and daughter when he died, and Copinger lost no time in securing the property. He married Dinah with immoderate haste and succeeded to the management and control of Galsham.

Once ensconced, Copinger's evil nature broke out like a wild beast uncaged. The house became a den for every wild fellow on the coast from Bideford to Land's End. Uproar and revelry filled the house by day and night, scandalising the neighbourhood and terrifying the womenfolk. Copinger soon organised a band of villains – smugglers, wreckers, footpads and pirates – to embark upon a complex system of crime and unlawful venture.

Strange vessels appeared off the coast, and signals flashed from cliff and headland to lead them to hidden creeks and sheltered coves. Tubs, kegs, casks and chests bursting with contraband goods were landed, for this was the heyday of smuggling, when vast profits were made by avoiding the customs duty placed on brandy, gin, tobacco, tea, silk and lace. It was said that no revenue officer or exciseman dared to be too vigilant west of the Tamar, while the poor country clergymen were either cowed by the brutality of the smugglers or had a hand themselves in the storing of contraband.

Copinger's ship, the *Black Prince*, was the terror of the seas from Hartland Point to the Lizard. A full-rigged schooner with a black hull, with Copinger in command she had once lured a revenue cutter into an intricate channel near Gull Rock. Due to Copinger's extensive knowledge of those waters she had escaped, but the king's ship perished with all those on board. However, it wasn't only smuggling that the *Black Prince* pursued. On 23 July 1779 the merchant brig Union, on her way from Boscastle to Bristol, was taken by the *Black Prince* off the coast at St Gennys and for this we have the written record of the Master of the Union, John Trick, who states that the brig herself was later ransomed for £200. This was an act of open piracy on the high seas.

Even worse was the practice of wrecking in which the 'Cruel' gang engaged. Many a brave ship was lured onto the rocks of that dangerous coast by false lights tied to the nodding head of a donkey being led along the cliff-top which, looking like a ship's bobbing stern-light, gave the illusion of there being plenty of sea-room. Once wrecked, any crew member or passenger who reached the shore was cruelly slaughtered by the gang on the grounds that 'dead men tell no tales'. Nor could landsmen expect mercy if they crossed Copinger's path. They were killed outright or abducted and forced to serve as crew. In 1835 an old man of ninety-seven told the Revd R.S. Hawker that he had been kidnapped by the 'Cruel' gang because he had happened to see one man kill another. After two years before the pirates' mast he was ransomed by his friends for a large sum of money. This was the first time he had mentioned the incident, so great was his fear of the evil Dane.

All over the countryside were byways and bridle paths that no man dared use at night, for they were Copinger's Tracks, the secret routes by which smuggled and stolen goods were distributed. Many of these tracks converged at a headland called Steeple Brink, a sheer cliff falling 300ft to the rocks below. 100ft down was an entrance to a vast and gloomy cave as big as Kilkhampton Church. This was Copinger's Cave, accessible only by a rope ladder lowered from above. In this cave they stored the loot: kegs of spirits, chests of tea and tobacco, bales of French silk, satin and lace. There were sheep and cattle in there too, fed on stolen hay and corn until their flesh was wanted for a feast, for here serious debaucheries took place; wild carousals and fierce revelries inconceivable, says Hawker, to the educated mind of the nineteenth century but not, I fear, to ours. Half-naked doxies brought up from Plymouth clad only in the lace fripperies of the brothel, strong spirits running like water, raucous music, savage dancing and barbarous games – it just sounds like an ordinary night out in Bideford or Barnstaple nowadays.

Of course, it is not to be supposed that the household at Galsham remained a happy one, for they had welcomed a monster into their midst; a man who had changed from the romantic, mysterious stranger who had leaped ashore in the storm to the very devil incarnate, a brutal villain so steeped in blood and crime that he was known throughout the country as 'Cruel Copinger'. He exercised a foul tyranny at Galsham, where everyone in the house, on the farm and for miles around was terrified of him.

Once, when a daring troop of excisemen visited Galsham, Copinger ordered Dinah to conceal a quantity of smuggled silk in the oven, while he showed the officers round some empty barrels in the cellar. When the officers left, having found nothing, Copinger discovered that the silk had been scorched, the oven having been used for bread-making and thus rendering the material unsaleable. He was so furious, he dragged the screaming Dinah into the bedroom and tied her to one of the pillars of the oak bedstead. Then he called his mother-in-law into the room and explained to her that it was his present intention to flog Dinah with the cat o' nine tails he held in his hand until all the skin had been taken from her back, unless her mother signed over to him everything left to her in Mr Hamlyn's will. This amounted to a considerable amount of money, property and other effects, including jewels, for it wasn't enough for Copinger to be in possession of the house and farm with all the stock and fields and revenue therefrom; he was in sore need of ready cash and this novel method of raising it proved most effective.

Meanwhile poor Dinah was with child – unimaginable their lovemaking! But the birth of a child brought no gladness into that home, for although the boy was healthy and well-formed and grew into a handsome, fair-haired child with his father's fine, flashing eyes, he was not only deaf and dumb but savage and evil from the moment of his birth. He was intensely cruel to animals, birds, other children and any living thing he could get hold of. He haunted the rocks along the shore with jabbering cries and spasmodic gestures and one day, when he was six years old, he was found at the edge of a tall cliff, beside himself with joy and pointing down to the beach, squirming and giggling with delight. Down there they found the mangled body of a neighbour's child, of about his own age, who had been his one constant companion when no other child would go near him and whom he had hurled over the cliff in some fit of savage glee. This spot was afterward his favourite haunt. He would draw passers-by to the place and point down, laughing horribly, but it did not do for the passer-by to venture too close to the edge.

It was said in that wild border country that Copinger's child had been born without a human soul as a judgement on the father's cruelty, but Copinger did not seem to mind this idea. On the contrary, he took delight in the boy's savagery, actively encouraging him in his evil propensities and the boy lived to be the pestilential scourge of the district.

Cruel Copinger blatantly mocked any attempt to restrain his wickedness. Once the vicar of Stratton, a meek and mild man, had spoken openly of the vile practices in the cave, in words of gentle condemnation, mentioning also that Copinger never paid his tithes. This aroused the devil's wrath. The vicar was jogging homeward one day from his parish rounds on his old cob and had reached the middle of the desolate heath bordering Herstridge Wood, when he heard the clattering of hooves and a demonic yell behind him. Down upon him rode Copinger on the terrible mare that none could ride but him (of course!) and in the next instant the vicar felt a searing pain on his back, as Copinger landed a terrific blow with his cat o' nine tails. The vicar was mercilessly flogged all the way home, unable to escape on his rambling old cob, and when he staggered in at his door, the clothes ripped from his body, his back stripped and bleeding, he heard Copinger sneer, 'There's your damned tithes, parson, and never mind the receipt!'

Copinger's fearful mare looms large, black and satanic in another adventure. The Cruel gang was carousing at the Hoops Inn at Horns Cross, when Copinger spotted a little old tailor sitting by the hearth. This was a half-witted, harmless old fellow known as Uncle Tom Tape, who went round from house to house mending clothes.

'Now then, Uncle Tom,' cried Copinger, 'we go the same road, so I'll give you a lift!' And, despite the old man's feeble protests, Copinger threw him up on to the crupper of his great black mare, mounted himself and galloped off into the night at breakneck speed. On and on they sped through the pitch-black darkness, the little tailor shrieking in terror until he pleaded to be told where they were going, upon which Copinger snarled back, 'I've promised my brother the Devil that I'll bring him a tailor to do his mending for eternity'. The tailor went into such a spasm of fear that he fell off onto the roadside, where they found him next morning muttering, 'No, no, no, no, no, that I'll never do. I'll never so much as thread a needle for Copinger's brother'. And that was all he ever said until he died, which was not long afterward.

☙

In his heyday Copinger bought a freehold farm bordering on the sea, Pentire-Glaze on Pentire Head, near Polzeath. This is the setting for Baring-Gould's fine romantic novel about Copinger, *In the Roar of the Sea*, in which Dinah is a more robust heroine than she is in the legend. It is said that on the day of the transfer of Pentire-Glaze, the astonished lawyer acting for the former owners was visited in his office in Wadebridge by Copinger and a crony, each carrying several large money bags. These were emptied out onto the desk and there lay heaps of foreign coins – dollars, ducats, doubloons, louis d'or, pistoles, sequins, golden guineas – the coinage of every nation on earth. After a small amount of argument and a great many oaths, the lawyer agreed to take it by weight. The document with Copinger's signature was said to be still extant in 1870. It was written in 'stern, bold, fierce characters, as if every letter had been stabbed upon the parchment with the point of a dagger', as R.S. Hawker, the vicar of Morwenstow puts it in his vivid account of Copinger. Underneath, in the same writing, is the strange word, 'Thuro'.

The end, though, was near. More and more revenue cutters were plying up and down the coast; the *Black Prince* was sunk in a running battle off Newlyn; money was scarce; and foreigners came to Galsham with news of an unknown danger.

One day at dusk, just as the sun was going down and a violent tempest was roaring up from the south-west, a wrecker, who had gone to Marsland Mouth to watch the shore, saw a strange vessel of foreign rig standing out to sea. A rocket hissed up from the Gull Rock and was answered by a gun from the ship, the puff of smoke coming a second before the dull boom of the cannon. All at once a well-known, much feared figure stood on the rock, the blood-red light of the dying sun flashing from the steel of his slowly waving sword. A boat put off from the ship, two hands at each oar to combat the deadly currents, and rode the heaving seas perilously close to the rock. The Herculean figure leapt into the boat and the rowers, bending to the oars like chained giants, battled through the boiling seas back to the ship. Once the tall figure and his men were on board, the ship seemed to vanish in the darkening light and worsening weather – a ghost ship sailing back to hell.

Thunder, lightning and hail crashed around the house at Galsham. Trees were torn up by the roots. Dinah watched the fury of the tempest from what she imagined was the safety of the sitting room, holding her poor, savage idiot-boy in her shuddering arms, more to keep him in the house than to comfort him, for the boy delighted in the storm, laughing with savage glee, and would have run out in it. Suddenly a meteor or stormbolt crashed through roof and ceiling into the very room where they stood, smashing Cruel Copinger's great leather armchair to smithereens. Exulting, the boy screamed, 'Father!', his first and only word and fainted in his mother's arms from the sheer passion of his emotions. They never saw Cruel Copinger again and no one mourned his passing. All that is left of him is the verse of a ballad:

> Will you hear of the Cruel Copinger?
> He came from a foreign kind:
> He was brought to us by the salt water,
> He was carried away by the wind.

This is the legend. The truth is less lurid and more prosaic. A man called Daniel Herbert Copinger was shipwrecked at Marsland Mouth on 23 December 1792 and he married Ann Hamlyn of Galsham, who was then forty-two, on 3 August 1793 at Hartland Parish Church. The marriage certificate, which can be found in the County Record Office in Exeter, states that Daniel Herbert Copinger was in the Royal Navy but there is no record of a Copinger in the Navy List at that time, nor of a naval vessel being wrecked at Marsland Mouth.

In 1802 Daniel Herbert Copinger was made bankrupt and imprisoned in the King's Bench Gaol. When he got out he lived in Barnstaple on an allowance from his wife, from whom he was

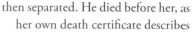

then separated. He died before her, as her own death certificate describes her as a widow. She died on 31 August 1833 and was buried next to her mother in Hartland Church.

Then there was John Copinger, a merchant of Roscoff in Brittany, who was one of the smugglers' main suppliers and who may have smuggled himself; he was said to have been in the British Secret Service at the time of the French Revolution.

There were other Copingers too who had murky pasts. Somehow, out of them all was woven the legend of Cruel Copinger and I have pieced it together from the writings of R.S. Hawker, the vicar of Morwenstow (who was quite a character in his own right) and Antony Hippisley Cox, whose book about smuggling in the West Country is well worth reading.

Twenty-nine

Witches

THE WITCHES OF ASHREIGNEY

In the *Transactions of the Devonshire Association*, Vol. 14, 1882, there are accounts of three witchcraft cases occurring in the parish of Ashreigney in the 1820s. These were called 'A Budget of Witch Stories' and were collected by Paul Q. Karkeek, who read them at Crediton in July 1882. They were told to him by a clergyman who heard the stories from his own grandfather, who had married the younger of the farmer's two daughters in the first story.

Bridge Farm, in the hamlet of Bridge Reeve, lies close to the River Taw in the parish of Ashreigney and in the 1820s it belonged to a Mr B---, one of the main farmers in the district. He had a wife and two daughters and the farm was a prosperous one, covering many acres, and with a lot of livestock.

At harvest time Mr B--- held a great reaping day, as was the custom then, to which people from all around would come to help with the work and share in the feast that followed. To this final cutting of the wheat came a man named Bowden and his wife, both of whom were reputed to be witches and therefore normally avoided; but as they made a point of attending all the local reaping days, they could not well be excluded. The cider flowed copiously all day, as was also the custom, for it was part of the farm labourers' wages then, a barrel being placed in the field for general use, and by suppertime Bowden and his wife were drunk and Bowden was belligerent. He thought he deserved a second helping of meat but instead of passing his plate along the table, he sent it whizzing over the surface toward the head of the table, where the farmer's wife was dishing out, breaking three other plates as he did so. The farmer's wife was furious and shouted at him, 'What did 'ee 'ave to do that for, you witching old rogue?!' Bowden lurched up from the table with a terrible oath and stumbled toward the farmer's wife, obviously with violent intentions, but the other men caught hold of him and bundled him to the ground. He lashed out at them and his wife joined in the fray but they were overpowered and thrown off the premises. As they left, they both swore a terrible revenge.

That night in bed the farmer and his wife expressed their fears to each other about the likelihood of such a revenge, given all the bad rumours about the Bowdens, and they did not have long to wait. The next day all the hens laid eggs with soft shells and in the days that followed the poultry fell about as if their backs were broken. Mysterious illnesses afflicted their sheep, cows, pigs and oxen. Every night animals would die, sometimes two or three at a time. Some of the animals died in extremely bizarre ways.

One day Mr B--- came back from Crediton market in the horse and trap and turned it loose into the stable while he went into the house, where he sent a lad out to attend to the horse. The boy came out of the stable having found no trace of it. He called his master and along with several other apprentice boys they made a careful search all over the farm for the missing horse, but didn't find it that night. It was found dead next day in a quarry three miles away, with its nearside front and back legs thrust through a single stirrup iron above the fetlock, both legs being hideously crushed and mangled. They sent for a blacksmith to remove the stirrup but he couldn't budge it, except by filing it off. He then tried to thrust a single hoof through the other stirrup-iron but couldn't. The smith, William Parker, kept the stirrup-iron as a curiosity until the day of his death.

Next day at dawn the men went into the shippen to feed the oxen and found one of them dead, a heavy ox-yoke stuck to the top of its horns. A day or two later, two of the oxen were found in their shed, their necks jammed and mangled together into a single yoke and the yoke properly fastened. These losses went on for months but Mr B--- did not believe in witchcraft, though everyone said he should; but when nearly his whole stock was wiped out, his wife and his men persuaded him to go and consult the local white witch up at Barnstaple. When he described what had happened and who was suspected, the white witch, or 'wise man' as they preferred to be called, said, 'By the time you get home, something else will be ill. It'll die but it's the last thing you'll lose'. Then he told the farmer what to do with it, which we shall learn in due course.

The farmer went home, stabled his horse and went to inspect a certain beautiful and valuable calf, which he was told was ill. As he looked in on the beast in its byre, it gave such a violent and unnatural leap that it struck a beam 6ft above its head and fell down dead. The farmer lost no time in carrying out the wise man's instructions. He cut out its heart, stuck it all over with pins and thorns, then took it that night to the quarry where the horse was found and burnt it. While this was being done, the wise man had said, something on the farm would start bleeding; and indeed, while the farmer was burning the calf's heart in the quarry:

> His two daughters were asleep together in the same bed in the farmhouse. The younger awoke and found that her feet were quite wet. She struck a light and discovered that her sister's leg had burst out bleeding and that she was all but dead from exhaustion and loss of blood. The doctor was fetched and he managed to stop the bleeding but the leg was never sound afterward. Some of this blood was sent to the white witch in Barnstaple and that was the end of their troubles.

The cure seems to have been almost as disastrous as the bewitchment. Presumably the white witch conjured with the daughter's blood and this, together with the burning of the calf's heart, put paid to the Bowdens' witchcraft and Bridge Farm was free.

This near-fatal bleeding in the service of white witchcraft was not the elder daughter's last experience of the black arts. She married a local farmer whose farm lay just outside Ashreigney. In the village itself lived an old woman whom the other villagers avoided, as she was thought to be a witch and it was believed that she could only have power over those that did business with her.

One day the farmer came in from the fields for his lunch and found his wife selling butter and eggs to the old woman. He went into a rage, forbade his wife to sell her anything again and ordered the old woman out of his house. She went, swearing that he'd regret it. His cattle began to die in the same strange ways as in the first story and he went to consult the same white witch in Barnstaple. This man stopped the bewitchment – we're not told how, but it probably involved hearts and pins – and said that the witch would bear a mark to her grave as a public warning to all. Shortly afterward, the old woman's right eye wasted away in a continuous discharge of noisome matter, frightful to see, so unsightly that she had to wear a green eyeshade over it and she was blind in that eye to the end of her days.

This old woman had a beautiful daughter who was courted by several local men, including a young mason called Will Ford but, as people grew still more afraid of her mother, the young man jilted the daughter and went no more near them, saying openly that he would not marry a damned witch's whelp. Shortly after this he fell down a well and broke both his thighs. He didn't die but was crippled for life and everyone said it was the result of the witch's ill-wishing. The girl herself, shunned and disheartened, pined away in a rapid consumption and on her death bed neighbours heard her say, 'Oh, mother, you drew the circle for Will Ford, and I have walked into it, and now I am dying'. Soon after she died and her mother did not survive her for long.

As stated at the start of this chapter, the clergyman's grandfather, Mr M---, married the younger of the two sisters and took over Bridge Farm. They employed a man called Durke who did odd jobs on the farm, mending hedges and the like, and who took his wages in kind – eggs, butter, vegetables, etc., keeping an account on a slate and settling up once a month. This man Durke and his wife and his widowed sister-in-law, Deb Knight, were all believed to be witches.

One day old Deb Knight was sent by Durke to make up the account – to get what they were owed by way of produce in lieu of wages – and started arguing with the farmer's wife, Mrs M---, about the amount of potatoes they'd had. The argument got so heated that the couple's little three-year-old boy, who was sitting on a stool near the fire, tumbled off into it in a fright and was badly burned. The mother, snatching the child up, cried out, 'You wicked old hussy! You've witched the child into the fire!' Deb Knight stormed off, shouting, 'I'll let you know if I'm a witch or not before three months are out!'

In a very short time the pigs got the staggers, dying at the rate of two or three a day, until every one of them, fifty or so, were dead. Then horned cattle, sheep and lastly horses sickened and died, until they'd lost more than £500 worth of beasts. Grandfather M--- was a very religious man and would not believe that witchcraft was at work until he was persuaded by his father-in-law, Mr B---, that this was the only explanation. He then accompanied Mr B--- to see another white witch called Old Baker, who lived thirty miles away near Tiverton.

As soon as Grandfather M--- entered the wizard's cottage, Old Baker looked up and said, 'Well, farmer! So you've come at last, now you've lost nearly all you had. Why not before? I would have stopped it'. Then he looked at some books and said, 'There are three that are injuring you. On your way home you shall see them in the guise of three hares coming out of a gutter-hole. You must take the heart of the next animal that dies, stick it full of pins, salt it and bury it'.

Mr M--- and Mr B--- started for home and at the exact place they were told they saw three large hares creep out of a gutter-hole, trot on before them for about half a mile, then disappear into the hedge. Mr M--- did as he was told and as soon as he had buried the salted heart stuck all over with pins, he lost no more stock and gradually the farm recovered, but it took a good few years.

What happened to Durke and his wife and his sister-in-law we are not told, but usually the witchcraft that had been confounded rebounded on the ill-wishers so they probably had a hard time of it, at the very least.

In a trial at Taunton in 1823 an alleged witch accused a neighbour of assault. The neighbour said she had consulted Old Baker, who had advised her to draw the witch's blood and so 'draw out' her power.

'Who the devil is Old Baker?' the judge wanted to know.

'Oh, my Lord,' said the woman, 'he is a great conjuror, the people say. He is a good deal looked up to by the poor people of these parts'.

'I wish we had the fellow here', said Mr Justice Burrough. 'Tell him, if he does not leave off his conjuring, he will be caught and charmed in a manner he will not like'.

THE WITCH OF MEMBURY

This story was also presented to the Devonshire Association by Paul Q. Karkeek in 1882, from an account told to him by an elderly nurse who had been serving maid on the farm in question when she was eleven years old and had personally witnessed the events.

Membury is a little village a few miles to the north of Axminster and nearby lay the farm of a Mr P---, a prosperous farmer who lived there with his wife, his children and his brother. On land belonging to the farm stood the cottage or hut of an old woman called Hannah Henley who, unlike the usual description of a witch, was, according to the nurse:

> …always a pattern of neatness and cleanliness. She generally wore short petticoats, with a large white apron, white as the driven snow, a plaid turnover, and a satin poke bonnet. Cats she had in any number and of all colours. She was a good cook, famous for her apple dumplings and crowdy pies and kept her cottage neat and clean.

It was said, though, that she often turned herself into a hare, which the local harriers used to chase. Everyone was frightened of her, except the young serving maid and the farmer's brother, who were kind to her.

But Hannah was a cadger and as she lived so near the farm she was always calling there, asking for 'corn, bread, milk, flour, beer, sometimes money but she never asked like begging – she demanded'. They found her an embarrassing nuisance and at last grew tired, and one day the brother refused her money.

'You'll not live long to use it yourself', she replied and in three weeks he was taken ill and died in agony. After this, the farmer's wife refused to give Hannah anything more at all.

Not long after the brother's death, the maid was out walking with the youngest child when they came across Hannah. The little boy was playing with a walnut, which he offered to Hannah but the maid wouldn't allow it. Hannah stooped down and drew the sign of a cross in a circle in the dust of the road. The child was taken ill that night. He squatted on the floor and turned round and round very rapidly until he was giddy, a common sign of be-witchment, and this went on for four days until he died.

Now a reign of terror began. Hannah drew a circle with two sticks in front of a team of horses. They stepped into it and that night they were dead. She cursed the cows and they went blind and mad. She stood on a hedge and looked at some lambs in a field and they all turned head over heels without stopping until they died. 'The milk would not set, the butter could not be made, bread put to bake only ran about the oven'.

One day when Hannah called at the farm, the farmer's wife refused to see her and hid in the pantry, telling a servant to say she wasn't at home.

'Tell your missus,' said Hannah, 'that she shall not move out of the pantry now, even if she wishes'. And so it proved: the mistress was stuck and not even the farmer could pull her out. The farmer was so furious, he got his gun and chased the old witch out of the house, but when she dared him to shoot he could not pull the trigger.

Once she begged some barley off one of the manservants. He refused and that night eight horses were taken ill in the stables. Two had to be shot straight away and four died some days later.

Sheep died at the rate of eight or ten a day. The farmer faced ruin and so, being desperate, he fetched a white witch from Chard in Somerset to come and live in the farmhouse for a month and deal with the case. A bed was made up for him in the parlour and he slept there by day, working at dusk and through the night, circumambulating the farm and consulting his big black book. The young maidservant crept downstairs one night and peeped through the keyhole:

> I saw this man on his knees before his book, and sparks of fire flashing about the room. Next morning I told the mistress I thought the parlour had been on fire, but I was sharply reproved for my pains and told not to meddle again, lest something dreadful should happen to me.

The wizard said, 'Hannah Henley is the hardest case I have ever tackled'. He filled an iron pot with barley and water and kept it boiling. He hung six bullocks' hearts in the fireplace, two in the centre stuck with pins and the other four with new nails. As these slowly disintegrated, so did the witch's heart and she came to the house day after day, looking pathetic and ill, begging for food and relief and pleading that since a certain day she could get no rest. The wizard would not allow any relief to be given, in spite of the kind heart of the mistress, for if they had given in just a little, all his work would have been wasted and the witch's power would have been twice as strong.

As it was, she gave up and the farmer paid the wizard £100 – a lot of money in those days! But it was tantamount to murder. No one would now help her and she was living on 2s a week and a loaf of bread. She paid 6d for rent and 6d for snuff. The last time she was seen alive was Tuesday of Holy Week, when local huntsmen saw her struggling over a gate with a bundle of sticks. She asked for help but no one would go near her. On Maundy Thursday some local women went to her cottage as she was obviously dying, but she said to leave her alone at night as her going would be hard.

Next morning, Good Friday, they went back and found her dead, lying in the stream outside her cottage with a kettle beside her that she had been trying to fill.

The serving maid said she had been found high up in a tree and that her flesh was torn, as if by nails and that there was blood all over the cottage; but all this was merely local gossip and someone had made up the story that she had been struggling with the Devil and that he had dragged her through the broken window. It was also said that a box was found by her bed with a fair amount of money, tea, bread and sugar in it, and that two other boxes contained toads of various sizes. The serving maid said she was buried at a crossroads between Membury and Axminster. But all this was more gossip to cover up the shameful death of a lonely old woman whom no one would help.

The inquest stated that she had died of 'Water on the Brain', or apoplexy, which was likely to have caused delirium or hallucinations. She was buried in an unmarked grave in the churchyard. Local children pointed out her grave to Theo Brown and all that remains of her cottage are a few decrepit apple trees on the slope leading down to the stream. Was she really a witch or did the farmer simply blame her for a series of catastrophes with which he was mysteriously afflicted? We'll never know.

THIRTY

THE DEVIL'S FOOTPRINTS,
OR THE GREAT DEVON MYSTERY

Not all supernatural folklore has to do with witches and ghosts, but the Devil does seem to have had a special interest in Devon. 'The Devil's Footprints or the Great Devon Mystery' was a peculiar phenomenon well and widely recorded in its day and still unexplained to this day.

The winter of 1854-55 was a hard one and the night of 7/8 February 1855 saw a light fall of snow, followed by a slight thaw and a sharp frost (an 'ammel frost' as it's known in Devon), which made the snow turn to a treacherous layer of ice.

Next morning the Devonians to the south of Exeter and all around the Exe estuary looked out of their windows, and then came out of their houses, to see an apparently endless track of what looked like the hoof prints of a small donkey stretching over gardens and fields for miles and miles.

Some curious people followed the tracks. Every mark was exactly the same and they went in a dead straight line, keeping exactly 8½in apart. The tracks did not stop for any obstacle. If they came to a wall they simply continued on the other side, as if whatever it was had walked straight through. A shed was entered at the back wall and the footprints started again at the front. Houses were walked over. You could see the hoof prints going over the rooftops, up one side to the ridge and down the other. Low bushes were walked under and a 6in-diameter drainpipe was apparently walked through.

A young man called D'Urban, aged nineteen, from Clyst St Mary, later the first curator of the Royal Albert Memorial Museum in Queen Street, Exeter, pieced together the reports and rumours and made drawings of the hoof prints. The tracks seemed to start at Totnes, then travelled north and east, passing through Torquay, Teignmouth, Dawlish, Starcross, then across the Exe estuary, which was frozen over, to Topsham, Lympstone, Exmouth, Littleham and Woodbury. This detailed account was published in the *Illustrated London News* of 24 February.

The Revd G.M. Musgrave of Withycombe, near Exmouth, warned his congregation the following Sunday that Satan was ever ready to cross their path, but that in his opinion the marks were made by an escaped kangaroo. Oddly enough there was a Mr Fish at Knowle in Sidmouth who had a pet wallaby which did escape around that time, but it's difficult to see how a wallaby could have jumped a 14ft wall, squeezed through a 6in-diameter drainpipe or left clear footprints on a second-storey windowsill. Anyway, the marks were nothing like those made by a wallaby or a kangaroo.

On 3 March the Revd Musgrave defended himself in the *Illustrated London News* – which seems to have particularly taken up the story – with the words:

> I certainly did not pin my faith to that version of the mystery, or call upon others to believe it 'ex cathedra'; but the state of mind of the villagers, the labourers, their wives and children, and old crones, and trembling old men, dreading to stir out after sunset, or to go out half a mile into lanes and byways, under the conviction that this was the Devil's work – rendered it very desirable to disperse ideas so derogatory to a Christianised, but assuredly most unenlightened, community.

Woolmer's Exeter & Plymouth Gazette, in their 17 February issue, suggested that 'the poor are full of superstition and consider it little short of a visit from Satan or some of his imps', especially as some of the prints looked decidedly cloven.

Some people from Dawlish armed themselves with guns and clubs and followed the prints all day but returned in the evening no wiser than they had set out. One report, by a Londoner visiting Devon at the time, said that the tracks were followed by hounds and huntsmen and a mob of country folk until, at last, in a wood above Dawlish, the hounds came back baying and terrified; as no one was brave enough to investigate, they all went home. But that was written by a Londoner so what can you expect?

There is little evidence, in fact, to suggest that the tracks started further west than Teignmouth, although Theo Brown's father thought the creature, whatever it was, had crossed the River Dart and had come from as far west as Bolt Head, while an item in her grandfather's scrapbook says, 'On a winter's morning the men on the estate were startled at the discovery of strange footprints in the snow: the "cloven foot" was the general remark along the countryside'. The estate in question was the Barton Hall estate which at that time extended as far as the coast at Watcombe.

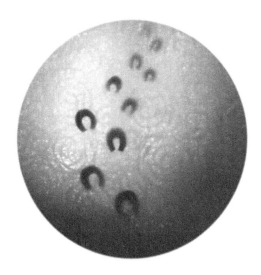

The Revd H.T. Ellacombe, vicar of Clyst St George, made careful drawings of the tracks and discovered that they were not continuous. Sometimes they appeared suddenly in the middle of a field, so that it seemed as if birds with ice on their feet might be a partial solution, especially as some of the prints had little flurries at the front, suggesting claws. But again, this does not tally with the majority of the marks, which look distinctly like horse-shoes or cloven hooves, and donkeys are the only animals that plant their feet in an almost perfectly straight line, one in front of the other. In the 1970s a naturalist suggested that the marks were like those made by a short-tailed field vole squatting in snow.

The marks at Woodbury, however, were clearly made by practical jokers with a hot horse-shoe pressed firmly down to the ground. No single explanation has ever covered all the known and reported facts, but I am personally inclined to the theory of a gang of practical jokers stationed at intervals across the county, two or three people being responsible for an area and sworn to secrecy, rather like the modern artists and con merchants that make crop circles. People are ready and willing to believe in almost anything.

There have been other mysterious tracks reported from all over the world, while even just in England, at the same time as the Devon Mystery, there was the report of another track being laid from Dorset to Lincolnshire and a Dartmoor man said a track came down from North Devon right across the Moor to the south side.

In 1955 Theo Brown was talking to a group of people at Ipplepen about the Great Devon Mystery, when they told her that mysterious footprints had been seen that February at a house in the village. It was a very old house, L-shaped and thatched. The lady of the house noticed that it was snowing heavily and was worried about her roof-beams holding the weight, so she went out to see how thick it was. It was about 4in deep and then she saw a steady single track similar to that made by a lady's shoe going up across the roof, over the ridge and down the other side. When she went back indoors, her two dogs, a Golden Labrador and a Boxer, were terrified and refused to come into the kitchen.

Two hours later the dogs relaxed and were perfectly normal. Two other people saw the footprints, 100 years to the very day after the Great Devon Mystery!

One last mystery. As Theo Brown finished reading two papers on the Devil's Footprints to the Devonshire Association, in which she quoted the Revd Ellacombe's careful and meticulous reports, a member told her that the long-deceased vicar had been seen lately in the vicarage drive at Clyst St George. The person who saw him possessed his portrait and knew exactly what he looked like, so there is a ghost connected to the Great Devon Mystery after all; but I still think the footprints themselves were a hoax.

Oddly enough, the very day I wrote this story, there was an article relating to the Devil's Footprints in the *North Devon Journal Herald*, stating that strange footprints were seen in the recent snow around Woolfardisworthy. The Great Devon Mystery is alive and well!

BIBLIOGRAPHY

S. Baring-Gould, *Devonshire Characters and Strange Events* (John Lane, The Bodley Head, London, 1908)

Mrs Bray, *The Borders of the Tamar and the Tavy* (Kent & Co., London, 1879)

Theo Brown, *Devon Ghosts* (Jarrold, Norwich, 1982)

J.R.W. Coxhead, *Devon Traditions & Fairy Tales* (The Raleigh Press, Exmouth, 1959)

William Crossing, *Folklore and Legends of Dartmoor* (Forest Publishing, 1997)

A Farquharson-Coe, *Devon's Ghosts* (James Pike Ltd, 1975)

R.S. Hawker, *Footprints of Former Men in Far Cornwall* (Westaway Books Ltd, London, 1870)

John Pegg, *After Dark on Dartmoor* (John Pegg Publishing, 1984)

Deryck Seymour, *Berry Pomeroy Castle* (Deryck Seymour, Torquay,1982)

V. Day Sharman, *Folk Tales of Devon* (Thomas Nelson & Sons Ltd, 1952)

Ruth E. St Leger-Gordon, *The Witchcraft and Folklore of Dartmoor* (Robert Hale Ltd, 1965)

T. Westcote, *View of Devonshire in 1630* (Edited in Exeter, 1845)

Jennifer Westwood & Jacqueline Simpson, *The Lore of the Land* (Penguin, 2005)

Ralph Whitlock, *The Folklore of Devon*, (Batsford, 1977)

Various, *Transactions of the Devonshire Association*